Robotics

What Beginners Need to Know about Robotic Process Automation, Mobile Robots, Artificial Intelligence, Machine Learning, Autonomous Vehicles, Speech Recognition, Drones, and Our Future

© **Copyright 2019**

All Rights Reserved. No part of this book may be reproduced in any form without permission in writing from the author. Reviewers may quote brief passages in reviews.

Disclaimer: No part of this publication may be reproduced or transmitted in any form or by any means, mechanical or electronic, including photocopying or recording, or by any information storage and retrieval system, or transmitted by email without permission in writing from the publisher.

While all attempts have been made to verify the information provided in this publication, neither the author nor the publisher assumes any responsibility for errors, omissions or contrary interpretations of the subject matter herein.

This book is for entertainment purposes only. The views expressed are those of the author alone, and should not be taken as expert instruction or commands. The reader is responsible for his or her own actions.

Adherence to all applicable laws and regulations, including international, federal, state and local laws governing professional licensing, business practices, advertising and all other aspects of doing business in the US, Canada, UK or any other jurisdiction is the sole responsibility of the purchaser or reader.

Neither the author nor the publisher assumes any responsibility or liability whatsoever on the behalf of the purchaser or reader of these materials. Any perceived slight of any individual or organization is purely unintentional.

Contents

INTRODUCTION 1
CHAPTER 1: THE BASICS OF ROBOTICS 2
CHAPTER 2: FIVE REASONS WHY EXPERTS WARN US ABOUT ROBOTS 17
CHAPTER 3: TEN MYTHS ABOUT ROBOTS 23
CHAPTER 4: EVERYTHING YOU NEED TO KNOW ABOUT ROBOTIC PROCESS AUTOMATION 29
CHAPTER 5: MOBILE ROBOTS 33
CHAPTER 6: ARTIFICIAL INTELLIGENCE 45
CHAPTER 7: MACHINE LEARNING 61
CHAPTER 8: AUTONOMOUS VEHICLES 78
CHAPTER 9: SPEECH RECOGNITION 82
CHAPTER 10: DRONES 85
CHAPTER 11: ROBOTICS IN BUSINESS 90
CHAPTER 12: ROBOTICS FAQ 95
CHAPTER 13: MACHINE LEARNING AND ARTIFICIAL INTELLIGENCE 103
CONCLUSION 107

Introduction

The following chapters will discuss everything that you need to know about robotics. As you look at the world around us, more and more robotics has been applied to our lives.

Because of how important robotics is becoming in our lives, it is important that you understand how robotics works and some of the myths that are often told about robotics.

There are many topics in this book, and you will read about some of the experts and what they have to say about robotics. It is important to understand everything about robotics before you decide to write it off as a hoax or something worse.

Chapter 1: The Basics of Robotics

Robotics is considered an exhaustive branch of science and engineering. Robotics encompasses different fields of engineering such as electronics, information, mechanical, computer science, and so much more! It is typically related to the use of robots, how they are invented, how they operate, and the computer system that is used to control the robot. It also includes feedback from sensors as well as the processing of information that the robot has to use.

The robotic technologies are used to create machines that are going to take the place of humans by replicating human actions. Robots can be used in many situations for any number of purposes. However, when you look in today's society, they can be used in dangerous environments that humans should not be in, such as the detection of bombs and even the deactivation of bombs. Robots can also be used in manufacturing processes where humans are not going to be able to survive because of space, air quality, or any other number of dangerous situations where humans are being placed in danger and are most likely not going to be able to survive. Robots can take on almost any form, and they can even be made to resemble what a human looks like. Doing this is said to help people accept robots as they replicate behaviors that are typically performed by people. Some robots can replicate hoisting, talking, walking, perception, and almost anything that a human can do. Many of the robots seen today are going to be inspired by the environment that they are going to be working in. These robots are going to contribute to nature because they are contributing to the bio-inspired field.

The concept of creating robots dates back to classical times. However, the research for it and the potential to create the perfect robot did not actually get put into action until the start of the 20th century. All across the course of history, people have assumed that robots are going to imitate human behaviors and handle tasks similar to how humans do every day. Now, you can see that robotics is a quickly growing field thanks to advances in technology.

Etymology

The word robotics comes from 'robot'. This word came to the public's attention by a Czech writer by the name of Karel Capek when his play was first published sometime in 1920. The origins of the word robot can be traced back to the Slavic word *roboa* which translates to labor or work. In Capek's play, it starts out in a factory that makes robots, and these creatures were mistaken for humans (the idea of androids). However, it was not Capek that made up the term robot, but he did write a letter in reference to the development of the word which was found in the Oxford English Dictionary stating that the word 'robot' was created by Josef, Capek's brother.

However, when you look at the Oxford English Dictionary, it tells you that the word 'robotics' was used first by Isaac Asimov in a science fiction story he wrote which was published in 1941. Asimov was not aware that he was creating a new word because of the technology and science that is seen in electrical devices. Therefore, he assumed that the word 'robotics' was going to only refer to the work that is done with robots. In his other works, Asimo says that it was a short story from 1942 when he first used the word 'robotics' where he first proposed the concept of The Three Laws of Robotics. But, since Liar predates Runaround by at least ten months, Liar is where the word first came about.

History

It was in 1948 that Norbert Wiener first created the cybernetics principles which are the basis for practical robotics.

The first fully autonomous robot made an appearance during the 20th century. The very first digital that was programmable was named Unimate, and it was put to use in 1961 so that it could remove the car pieces from the die casting machine so they could be stacked. Robots in both commercial and factory jobs are used worldwide today, and they can perform jobs cheaper while being more accurate and more reliable than a human being. They are also employed in jobs that are not going to be suitable for humans because they are too dull, dangerous, or dirty. Robots are typically used in mass production, fabrication, mining, transport, packing and packaging, surgery, the exploration of both Earth and space, safety, weaponry, and laboratory research.

Time Period	Name of the Inventor	Name of the robot	Significance
Before and third Century BC	Yan Shi		If you look at the Liezi text, you will see the earliest descriptions of automata. The text talks about a previous meeting between Yan Shi, a mechanical engineer, and King Mu of Zhou (1023-

				957 BC). A figure, shaped and sized like a human, was presented later to the king.
Before and first century AD	Heron of Alexandria, Philo of Byzantium, Ctesibius, and others			This describes more than a hundred automata and machines that include wind organs, fire engines, steam-powered engines, and coin-operated machines. They can be seen in the book which was written by Heron of Alexandria entitled Pneumatica and Automata.
C. 420 BCE	Archytas of Tarentum	Flying pigeon		Steam propelled a wooden bird which made it possible to fly.
1206	Al-Jazari	Hand washing automaton, automated moving peacocks, a robot band		A programmable early humanoid automata.

1495	Leonardo da Vinci	Mechanical Knight	A humanoid robot design.
1738	Jacques de Vaucanson	Digesting Duck	A duck made mechanically which can excrete, flap its wings, and eat.
1898	Nikola Tesla	Teleautomaton	A vessel controlled by radio was first demonstrated.
1921	Karel Capek	Rossum's Universal Robots	The play *R.U.R.* showed the first fictional automaton.
1930	Westinghouse Electric Corporation	Elektro	It was in 1939 and 1940 when the World's Fair first showed the humanoid robot.
1946		Whirlwind	The creation of the first general purpose digital computer.
1948	William Grey Walter	Elsie and Elmer	Biological behaviors can be observed in robots.
1956	George	Unimate	The company,

	Devol		Unimation, first created the commercial robot based on the patents of its creator.
1961	George Devol	Unimate	The installation of the first factory robot.
1967 - 1972	Waseda University	WABOT-1	The creation of the first android and the first full-scale humanoid intelligent robot. They can see and hear by using tactic sensors and can control their limbs. It can also communicate via an artificial mouth and the conversation system installed.
1973	KUKA Robot Group	Famulus	Six axes that were driven mechanically were used by the first factory robot.
1974	ABB Robot Group	IRB 6	A robot first guided the first microcomputer.

| 1975 | Victor Scheinman | PUMA | Unimation created a programmable universal manipulation arm. |
| 1978 | Patricia Ambler and Robin Popplestone | Freddy I and II, RAPT robot programming language | The robots are allowed to handle variations because of the sensors and the first object level robot programming languages. |

What are the experts saying about our future?

Roboticist Daniela Rus hopes to have a world where every person can have a robot despite where they fall on the economic ladder. Rus is the director of Computer Science and Artificial Intelligence Laboratory at the Massachusetts Institute of Technology (MIT) and has been reported saying that even though robotics has made major advancements, this dream is not yet possible.

"But just remember that only two decades ago, computation was a task reserved for few experts, because computers were large, expensive, and hard to use," Rus said. Now, everyone is using a computer, and that alone shows that technology can advance enough to bring artificial intelligence to the world.

Robotics is still in their infancy, but they are making advances every day.

Today, Amazon has more than 80,000 robots that are working in their fulfillment centers. Even with that many robots working for Amazon, the chief technologist for Amazon does not have any desire to replace humans with robots.

"Humans are really great at creative problem solving, abstraction, and generalizations. Robots are really good at crunching numbers, pulling data, lifting heavy objects, and moving with precision. We have to think about how we can build systems that bring the strengths of each of these components together." – Tye Brady.

Heather Ames from Neurala unveiled that they were working with Motorola Solutions where they were using artificial intelligence that can be used in finding missing children. The body cameras found on the uniforms of officers will receive the description of the missing child so that more people are looking for the child while they are lost. This same system is going to be applied to find suspicious packages.

Buddy Michini from Airware has stated that drones are going to be able to help first responders assess a catastrophic event. "They can take a drone for getting an overview of what's happening and put [help] at, say, the most crashed building." Michini also stated Airware sent their drones over to Italy to help with the most recent earthquake.

Robots are even placed on a human body to augment the skills that the human must use. This is being done so that they can restore the ability to anyone who has a physical impairment that they may have lost. The first use of these robots has been on soldiers so that they are not getting tired while they are carrying more than 100 pounds. The machine is not going to control the user, but instead, it is going to follow his moves. So, if they are stepping over rough terrain, it will combine the strength of the robot and the human so that they are working together.

How Robotics are being Used Today

Robots can be seen in the medical field today. They are so precise that they have become a great tool for surgery. Robots can do incisions that are much cleaner than a human being can do and once the cut is healed, it cannot be seen from a distance. Doctors no longer have to be scared of making the wrong incision or cutting too far into the patient. Robots can be programmed to cut in a specific place and to a certain depth. They have also been helpful in advancing medical discoveries and finding new information that can later help to save someone's life.

Robots can also be found in factories. They are used to weld cars and parts together. Because of how precise they are as well as their accuracy, it is easy to make their work appear as if a professional did the welding. The great thing about robots is that they are not bothered by the bright lights or heat from the welding torches either. Therefore, they can do more work than a human. The only downside is that they are going to require program updates to keep them going and up-to-date on the newest technology.

Robots have also been made for home entertainment and leisure. There is a variety of home robot kits that people can purchase. Some of these kits are going to make a robot that follows a line or traces a line. Other kits are going to make a robot that can determine if it is on the floor or the table and how far it can go before it hits something. These types of robots are going to have light sensors as well as switch sensors. There are even some robots that are going to be used for cleaning, such as to vacuum the floor or to serve other people. Pet robots are going to mimic pets while providing entertainment to the person that owns it. These pet robots can roll over, sit, and play with you.

Advantages of Robotics

Robots can be very helpful in our lives despite what people believe. Here are some ways that robots are helpful in our lives today:

1. Robots can perform tasks faster than humans, and they're consistent and accurate.
2. Robotic pets can help patients who are suffering from depression and can help to keep them active.
3. Most robots are automatic; therefore, they can move without interference from a human. This means that they can

entertain and perform specific tasks that are not safe for a human being.

4. Robots can be used to produce products and assemble cars. Robots can also be used when it comes to building parts for plans, cars, and construction equipment.

5. New jobs are being created to have people create and repair robots.

6. Since they are machines, robots can work without sleeping.

7. Robots can deal with hostile environments. Robots are created so that planetary atmospheres are not going to affect their performance nor will it affect their physical state. They can replace humans in many areas of work and can even program themselves to manage themselves better.

8. Robots can be programmed to navigate and reach the center of the Earth. They can dig for fuel and can be used in mining. Robots can also be programmed to explore the floor of the ocean and other parts where humans cannot go. Any limitations that humans have, robots can overcome.

9. Robots can be used when it comes to time-consuming and repetitive tasks. Robots are not going to get bored; therefore, they are not going to lose quality when it comes to their work. They can also do dangerous tasks that humans should not do. Their parameters for time and speed can be adjusted to make them react quicker. Robots can further be uninfluenced by the things that are going to affect humans negatively.

10. Robots can function without stopping. They can work without being serviced for an extended period of time as well as being able to work a long time without maintenance, which means that they have a higher production rate than most humans.

11. Robot hands will not tremble or shake as human hands do. Robots work with smaller and more versatile moving parts than humans. This is what makes them perfect for medical operations.

12. Robots are built so that they can work in the harshest of environments, such as space, underwater, or a fire. They can be used whenever a human's safety is called into question. Robots can also be created to come in any size that the task requires.

13. Robots are there to do jobs that people do not want to complete. Many robotic probes have been sent to space and never returned. They are built to be stronger than people. Robots have even been used in warfare to eliminate the need for putting people at risk.

Disadvantages of Robotics

Of course, robots are going to have their disadvantages as well:

1. Robots have to have 'power' to operate. People can lose their factory jobs, but even if they are replaced with robots, the robots will need to have maintenance to keep them running. It is going to cost a substantial amount of money to create and purchase robots. Plus, the programs and hardware that the robot is going to need will cost more money later on down the road.

2. Robots can take the place of a human in a factory. This means that people will need to locate a new job or they will have to be retrained to do a different job. In the event that robots replace humans in a variety of fields, this can lead to a high unemployment rate because not everyone can be trained to do maintenance on robots.

3. As stated, robots require maintenance and repair, which is going to cost money. Plus, their programs will have to be updated regularly because the requirements for the job may

change. The machines will have to be made to be smarter. In the event that there is a breakdown, the cost of repair is going to be high. This means that the procedures have to be restored, lost code of data recovered, and this can not only be costly but time-consuming as well.

4. Robots store a lot of data. However, getting access to the data is going to be harder than if you were pulling it out of a human brain. Robots are built to complete repetitive tasks, but they are not going to get better the longer that they do it like a human will.

5. Robots are not going to act in a way that is not already built into their programming. With how robots are being used today, people are going to easily be able to become dependent on machines which will end up causing them to lose control of their mental capacities. If the wrong hands took control of a robot, that robot could be used for destruction.

6. A robot is not intelligent or sentient. They cannot improve upon their jobs unless they are programmed to do so. They cannot think or have emotions. This severely limits how robots can assist or communicate with humans.

Real-world Applications

Robots are no longer science fiction; they are very real and in the world that we live in today. No, they are not trying to take over the world like some of the movies that we see, but they are working side by side with us and helping to improve our lives and making it so that we can improve the lives of those that we are working for. Below, you are going to see some real-world applications of robots and how they are helping make our world a better place:

1. *Bionic legs*: bio-mechatronics is a revolutionary work being done by Hugh Herr who is the head of the biomechatronics research group at MIT. Herr is a double amputee who used

human physiology with electro-mechanics to create a bionic limb for someone who has physical disabilities. His bionic achievements have included gait-adaptive knee prostheses for transfemoral amputees and a variety of impedance ankle-foot exoskeletons for gait pathology, which is also known as drop foot that can be caused by cerebral palsy, strokes, or multiple sclerosis. He has even done his own bionic legs which is the first foot and calf system.

2. *Hospital robots*: Atheon's focus is on the healthcare industry. By using autonomous mobile robots, they have helped with the transportation of heavy materials like laundry, clinical supplies, and cleaning products. On top of that, the TUG machines can safely remove hazardous waste. Being that regulations require that medical centers have to track all drugs, particularly narcotics, Aethon robots can deliver medicine as a part of an IOT (Internet of Things) scenario. Plus, it has RFID chips and barcodes on all the medicines that are going to enable it to track the medicines in real time.

3. *Robot valets*: Smart garage vendors like Boomerang can provide a unique approach to robotic garages. Robots are programmed to get your car and park it for you so that they can maximize the space that is inside the garage. Boomerang functions similar to an elevator with a service called Robotic Valet. These garages are primarily in locations where real estate is expensive, such as San Francisco, Miami, and Chicago.

4. *Parking lot robots*: Serva-TS works like a warehouse forklift that is going to shuffle vehicles through a parking lot like a deck of cards is shuffled. This system works in the Dusseldorf airport and can retrofit older garages by gaining 40 percent of usable space in the process.

5. *Factory robots*: Boston's Rethink Robotics introduced robots that can work alongside humans to do warehouse activities like pick and pack.

6. *Collaborative robots*: Denmark's Universal Robots have brought out a whole line of collaborative robots to the world market. These robots are programmable and are invented to handle repetitive tasks which help to free up people to do more advanced activities.

7. *Robotic factory painter*: ABB Robotics has come up with a line of robotic painters. There is a hollow wrist in IRB 580 that is compact and is a fast and accurate painting robot. This robot helps increase productivity and presents more efficiency to painting companies.

8. *Collaboration*: the KUKA systems have launched collaborative robotics that is meant to meet the needs of the growing market. This robot features sensory capabilities for safety, simple operator control, and faster teaching. There are a few applications to these robots that include inspection, testing, measuring, palletizing, machining, and fastening.

9. *Humanoid robots*: The Intelligent Robotics Laboratory's director, Professor Hiroshi Ishiguro, (the laboratory is part of the Department of Systems Innovation in the Graduate School of Engineering Science at the Osaka University in Japan) has created an android that goes by the name of Geminoid. Geminoid looks exactly like Professor Ishiguro.

10. *Humanoids helping humans*: Even though these robots look humanoid and are considered to be cute, they are not all invented to do household chores or entertain. Honda and Toyota created a walking assisted device for those that are physically impaired or elderly. Cyberdyne's HAL (Hybrid Assistive Limb) system is the only robotic device that can help to teach the brain how to move the limb that it is replacing. On top of that, the medical applications have full

body HAL systems that are going through research and development to enhance or protect the human body for situations like disaster recovery, harsh environments, or circumstances where humans need to have superior strength and endurance.

Chapter 2: Five Reasons Why Experts Warn Us about Robots

Some experts condone the use of robots and others do not. Then, some experts are somewhere in the middle:

1. *Elon Musk*: Elon Musk is a billionaire and a techpreneur who has been issuing warnings to the public when it comes to the dangers of artificial intelligence being used for military robots. There is rapid adoption of robot technology that is occurring in our society and the consequences that it will have on our society in the event that these robots are not secure. But what is the big deal if our robotics technology is not secure?

Well, robots are pretty much computers that can move. Therefore, if they are hacked, then the threat is going to be bigger than if a stationary computer is hacked. Whenever a stationary computer is hacked, the hacker is only able to steal information and use the system to hack other systems. However, whenever a robot is hacked, it can be used to harm other people and even kill them because it can move around. At the same time, some robots have cameras and microphones because they can be used as an espionage tool. Some people still believe that this can only happen in the movies or books, but the risks and threats are real, and there has already been evidence where robots have harmed people or destroyed property.

Take, for instance, the US Department of Labor that has a list of robot-related incidents that have led to a dozen deaths. Robotic surgery has been tied to 144 deaths in the US over the last 14 years. In 2016, a Chinese robot broke a glass window and hurt someone who was standing nearby.

The more intelligence, power, and functionality that a robot has, the bigger the threat is going to be. There was a video that was released from Boston Dynamics that showed a robot doing physical acrobatics which was to show off the company's advanced technology. Now, imagine that this technology got hacked. What would happen if a robot of this strength and intelligence was hacked and received malicious commands?

With this being said, it is easy for a friendly robot's security to be bypassed and for a robot that is helpful and was trusted to become malicious and harm property or people.

    2. *Stephen Hawking*: There have been more than 1,000 tech experts, researchers, and scientists that have composed a letter that states a warning about the dangers of autonomous weapons. This letter was signed by Apple's co-founder Steve Wozniak, Stephen Hawking, and Elon Musk.

The letter was presented at an international AI conference in 2015. It came about because out of control robots are the most recent topic for debate. It has been heatedly discussed by multiple committees at the United Nations when it comes to placing a ban on specific weapons that are autonomous.

Scientific experts have been trying to place a ban on artificial intelligence being used in weapons that can get out of human control. They even went on to add that just as chemists and biologists are not going to have an interest when it comes to building weapons of biological or chemical origins, the AI researchers are not going to be interested in building AI weapons and do not want other researchers to make a mockery of their field by creating these weapons.

Daniel Dennett, a consciousness expert, DemisHassabis, the chief of Google AI, and Noam Chomsky, MIT professor, have also endorsed the letter.

Professor Stephen Hawking stated, "humans, who are limited by slow biological evolution, couldn't compete [with artificial intelligence], and would be superseded."

> 3. *Dr. Ian Pearson*: Dr. Pearson is a self-proclaimed futurologist and an inventor who claimed that AI is eventually going to be smarter than humans by a billion times and that to merge with it is our best bet.

Pearson said, "We'll have trained [artificial intelligence] to be like us, trained to feel emotions like us, but it won't be like us. It will be a bit like aliens off *Star Trek* – smarter and more calculated in its actions. It will be insensitive to humans, viewing us as barbaric. So, when it decides to carry out its own experiments, with viruses that it created, it will treat us like guinea pigs."

In the end, it is what worried Elon Musk! This also ties into what we discussed about the AI being hacked and used to turn against its user. In the end, it sounds like something out of science fiction movie, but it is something that could happen! It is something that Elon Musk spends millions of dollars on to make sure that he is keeping tabs on all robotic technology to make sure it doesn't happen.

> 4. *Europe*: Earlier this year, Europe was considering providing robots that are more advanced in natural rights and responsibilities. This proposal was presented to Europe's top regulator, the European Commission.

There are over 150 professionals in medical science, ethics, law, robotics and artificial intelligence that weighed in on the debate.

In a letter that was sent to the European Commission, these experts stated that it looked as if the proposal was influenced not by the real world but more by science fiction.

Those against the proposal argued that if legal status were provided to advanced robots, it would make it to where they could be held accountable for any damage that they cause.

A commission spokesperson stated "Artificial intelligence can bring major benefits to our society and economy… but it also raises questions, for example, related to the impact of AI on our society and the future of work."

The experts who examined the proposal stated that it could allow manufacturers, owners, and technicians to claim that they were not responsible for their robots when they did something wrong.

Experts further argued that by granting legal status to a robot, it would be inappropriate and that this idea was thanks to science fiction and sensational press announcements that had been made earlier this year.

A robotics' ethics expert, Nathalie Nevejans, who worked in France's Artois University, was one of the experts to sign the letter. She says that robots having legal status are not only unhelpful but inappropriate. There is no chance that a robot can be part of society without a human operator, and that is not going to change anytime soon.

Nevejans has been reported saying, "the legal personality would blur the relationship between the man and the machine so that the legislator could progressively move towards the attribution of rights to the robot. This would be utterly counterproductive to the extent that we develop them to serve us."

Rules should be created for artificial intelligence and robotics by Europe, according to several professionals, in order to foster innovation and ensure the citizens' safety. However, a vision of a future where robotic overlords rule should not be the basis.

This proposal was part of Europe's attempt to be ready for what is to come. The resolution is written to say that robots will need to report to the authorities while the laws are written in a way to say that robots are supposed to help humans and better humanity while not causing damage.

However, the parliament ended up rejecting the proposal saying that if robots started to replace human workers, then their owners would have to pay tax or contribute to social costs.

5. *Prime Ministers of Australia and Canada*: There have been hundreds of experts that have called on governments to ban the weaponization of robots that have the capabilities to decide if a person should live or die.

Letters have also been sent by leading AI figures to their prime ministers for the Conference on the Convention on Certain Conventional Weapons which took place in November of 2017.

These letters were also endorsed by Stephen Hawking who, at Portugal's technology conference, sent out a warning that AI could destroy the world.

Some of the signatures on these open letters included Professor Ian Kerr from the University of Ottawa as well as Professor Tim Baldwin from the University of Melbourne.

Prime Minister Justin Trudeau of Canada stated, "Lethal autonomous weapons systems that remove meaningful human control from determining the legitimacy of targets and deploying lethal force sit on the wrong side of a clear moral line."

Each letter sent to Canada and the UK highlighted that the spectacular advances that have come from machine learning and artificial intelligence have led to machines being able independently to perform difficult operations without human intervention.

These advancements have helped lead to many improvements in education, transportation, health care, and infrastructures. However, positive transformations are also going to have dangerous outcomes, too, which are going to end up demanding heightened moral attention.

Autonomous weapon systems, as warned by robotic corporations, will be the representative of at least 1/3 of the warfare's revolution. So, to keep this from happening, to ban these systems, each letter sent to the UK and Canada is calling for a new international agreement.

Each letter concluded, "If developed, they will permit armed conflict to be fought at a scale greater than ever, and at timescales faster than humans can comprehend. The deadly consequence of this is that machines – not people – will determine who lives and who dies."

An international ban on landmines, The Ottawa Treaty in 1996, and this ban were compared to each other by Canada's Minister of Foreign Affairs.

Completely banning autonomous weapons may be impossible. However, if all countries cooperate, the ban will be effective.

"When it comes to a ban, I think it's impossible to have an international ban. It will be country-specific," Abishur Prakash told Newsweek. "Countries like Russia, China, and Iran may see an international ban as an attempt by the West to assert control. If these countries don't ban them, then countries like the United States and Canada would see a ban on killer robots as a threat to their own national security."

Chapter 3: Ten Myths about Robots

Robots are still misunderstood which means that there are going to be myths about them because people are going to be making up information to help themselves understand robots a little bit more. In this chapter, we are going to examine some of these myths and put them to rest so that you do not have to continue to wonder about robots, and thus, will be one step closer to understanding them.

1. *Robots will take jobs away from people*: Each major logistics and the manufacturing company believe that robots are going to improve the efficiency of their operations and the quality of life for those that are working there. Therefore, humans are going to keep being a key part of the business whenever it comes to robotics.

Workers in manufacturing and logistics companies should look at robots as craftsmen who use precision tools to enhance their output as they create greater satisfaction when it comes to the job that is being done. Tesla Motors is an example of a company that uses robots to do tasks that are going to be a threat to the humans working there. The workers oversee the operations of the robot and make sure that the quality of work that they are putting out is up to par and is what is expected from Tesla Motors. At Tesla Motors, the robots working on the assembly line glue, rivet, and weld automotive parts together all while being watched by a human. Each worker at Tesla can be proud of themselves because they are part of a new era in manufacturing where the robots are being used to revamp.

> 2. *Robots are expensive*: modern day household applications are going to be just a few pieces of household hardware that people purchase every day without a second thought. Each of these pieces of equipment has evolved thanks to decades of improvement and a million units in the field that have been developed which has spread the costs out. The same principle is applied to robots. The issue is that almost every robot is going to need to be specialized and will require hardware that is going to cost a lot.

The actuators are going to be one of the most expensive parts that a robot needs to have. The price of these actuators is not coming down like the price of processors or sensors. Take, for example, Willow Garage spinout factory Perception. Before it was bought out by Google, this startup got close to human speed when it came to spotting and removing boxes from containers.

Though, this robotic system uses sensors that are inexpensive like cameras or the Kinect devices that are built by Microsoft. However, the robot is still going to require an expensive robotic arm that has to be powered by conventional actuators. The good news is that there is a chance that we are about to see a lot of innovation when it comes to the actuation systems. It is going to help bring down the cost of robots as it did for appliances.

One of the very promising areas will involve the sensors that are placed on the joints which then allow the robot to control its motions in safe and calculated ways.

There are groups like Carnegie Mellon University's (CMU) spinout IAM robotics, Redwood Robotics, and Modbot that are searching for unique ways to reduce the number and simply the motors, gears, and sensors that a robot needs. By doing this, the price of robots is going to dramatically be reduced which will help to reduce the costs of the arms which will end up dominating the cost of the entire robot.

3. *High-level operations are what robots are supposedly used*: Like a CNC (Computer Numerical Control) machine, robots are programmable, where the robot will be changed over from one running reference to a different one through the process of calling on a new program. Thanks to careful designs, it is possible for flexibility to be incorporated into an entire family of parts through the end stage stimulus. If completely necessary, a robot can exchange their "hands" like that of a CNC machine which can change the tools that it needs to do its job.

The technology of sensors has already advanced, which allows it to simplify the part presentation. Vision systems can identify and locate parts as well as reduce the need for hand tools. Forced sensing helps robots adjust so that they can do assembly tasks that require precision.

More modern robots can be used effectively to handle up to medium volume manufacturing. Manufacturing robots are programmed and switched out quickly, which ends up resulting in high-speed economical production.

4. *The programming in robots is hard because of how complex they are*: Robots are programmed through programs offline or teach pendants. With the pendant, the person who is programming the robot is going to take the robot and will be sent through a series of steps as it is fine-tuned and stores every point that needs to be stored. The robot will then go through this program and check to see if there are any collisions before it runs through it again. It will continue to run through it until the person programming the robot is completely satisfied with the motion that is being taught and that it will run without any issues.

Offline programming means that the user can use a model to complete and modify any movements that will later be used by the robot. How well the model responds to the program is going to determine how many modifications it needs after it has been installed on the robot.

5. *Robot systems are complex, and the programs are difficult to support*: Robots are extremely reliable compared to other machines that are being used in commercial and factory settings. Robotics vendors have quoted an average time between failures at 62,000 numbers or more in about seven years. Robot cells are usually going to include other equipment on top of all the lower reliability sensors. However, overall, dedicated automated equipment will still be more complex than the cell.

6. *Robots do whatever I tell them to do*: Robots that are built to respond to voice commands are out there. However, they are far and few in between because the practical applications for it are limited. Right now, it is more efficient and cost-effective to program a robot and control them through automation. Therefore, in the end, this myth is plausible, but it is not practical right now.

7. *Robots are machines built to look like a human*: What a robot looks like is going to depend on the source of the robot. According to Merriam-Webster, the definition of a robot is "a machine that looks like a human being and performs various complex acts of a human being; also: a similar but fictional machine whose lack of capacity for human emotions is often emphasized."

There are other definitions for a robot, but in the end, the robot is going to be built to display a design that is going to be efficient for the work that it is doing.

8. *Robots are strong but they are not agile*: In 2015, researchers at Stanford Universty's Biomimetics and Dexterous

Manipulation Lab built a gecko-bot that could pull up to 2,000 times its weight which is the equivalent of a human pulling a whale across the land.

Of course, robots are going to be stronger than humans, but that does not mean that they are not as agile as humans.

The Ecole Polytechnique Federale in Switzerland invented a robotic gripper that could carry 80 times its weight and was dexterous enough to pick up an egg or a single piece of paper. This gripper was the first to use electroadhesion and sensors that would allow the robot to adapt to the situations that it was placed in.

Robots are starting to perform all kinds of fine motor skills that allow them to perform jobs that humans were doing, and they are doing so without pause.

> 9. *Robots are smart, but they cannot determine intent*: Robots are built to be smart enough to replace jobs that humans do every day, and it is predicted that by 2040, smart robots are going to outnumber humans.

AI bots can transcribe speech better than most professional transcribers, and they can also spot cancer on a tissue slide better than human epidemiologists. Artificial intelligence is even creating robots that can teach themselves to be smarter!

So, in turn, as a robot gets smarter and learns more, it is going to be able to learn intent and make themselves smarter.

> 10. *Robots can learn, but they cannot be self-evolved*: As you've seen, robots are strong and smart, but you may think that they cannot evolve. However, you're wrong.

A Norwegian robot learned how to self-evolve while 3-D printing the next generation of itself. Experts located at the University of Oslo said, "Where artificial intelligence programs – not humans – innovate new products."

In other words, because technology is constantly evolving, it means that there are going to be robots that are going to be able to self-evolve and get smarter than when they were first created.

As you can see, there are plenty of myths that have been proven false about robots, and there are plenty of other myths out there that still need to be disproven. So, just because you do not understand robots does not mean that you need to make up things about them. It is easier to go online and look for what you are want to know than to believe a lie and make yourself look like a fool when you are talking about something you are not an expert on.

Chapter 4: Everything You Need to Know about Robotic Process Automation

Robotic process automation is also known as RPA and is quickly emerging in the form of business process automation technology which is going to be based on the programs that robots and artificial intelligence work on.

In most traditional workflow automation tools, there is going to be a developer that will create a list of actions that have to be automated for a task to be completed while being interfaced to the back of the system through the use of an internal application program or API. It can also use dedicated scripting languages. This is going to be different because RPA systems will develop action lists by watching what users do and they will be placed in the application's graphical user interface before they execute the automation through repetition of the task directly in the GUI. This will be able to remove the barrier that will allow automation to be used in projects that that may not contain API for this reason.

RPA tools are going to have some of the same techniques that are seen in graphical user interface tools on a technical level. The tools can program the interactions that are tied to the GUI and usually do so by repeating the actions that were done by the user. RPA tools will be different from other systems which include features that can enable data to be dealt with between and during the running of several applications. Take for example, when you receive an email that has an invoice attached. The data can be extracted and then typed into a system that is going to keep track of the finances.

History of Evolution

RPA is noted as a major technological advancement, and it is because of this solution that it will require new program platforms that are coming out to be more mature, resilient, scalable, and even reliable when being used by large enterprises.

When you look at how far technology has come since screen scraping, you will be able to understand it better when you look at an example that is often cited in academic studies.

A platform that users use known as Xchanging – a global company based out of the UK which provides business processing, procurement services, and technology throughout the world – has an anthropomorphized robot that goes by the name Poppy.

From this example, the level of genius and how user-friendly it is to use, especially in some of the more modern technology platforms, can be seen. Because of this, users could see it not as a hypothetical programmed service, but as an entity or thing. Thanks to the code-free platform of RPA, it will be one of the biggest things that set RPA apart from screen scraping.

Deployment

Hosting RPA services is going to align with a metaphor for programmed robots where every robotic movement has its own workplace, similar to human workers. Robots can use the same controls that are seen on a computer to take action and execute tasks. Typically, these actions are going to occur in a controlled environment and not on a display because a robot is not going to require physical screens to see their outcomes. Instead, it will interpret the outcomes electronically so that they do not need to be displayed on a screen. If these modern solutions could not be deployed on a large scale, then its availability will be limited and can only manage a few physical hardware and associated costs. Implementing RPA into major enterprises has helped save a lot of money whenever it has been likened to the more traditional non-RPA solutions.

Of course, RPA has its hazards. Criticism includes the risk of suppressing creativity and can even end up making more complex maintenance environments out of the programs that already exist

The Impact of RPA on Employment

When you look at the Harvard Business Review and what they said about RPA, you will see that they believe most operations groups will adopt RPA while making a promise to those that work for them that robots are not going to result in unemployment. Rather, the workers will be retrained so that they can spend their time doing something more interesting. According to an academic study, workers shouldn't feel that automation is a threat to their knowledge, but acknowledge them as teammates. In the same study, you can also see that instead of resulting in a lower headcount, when technology has been deployed, there has been more productivity with the same number of people.

On the other hand, some analysts believe that RPA is going to be a risk to business processes that outsource their work. This will create high-value jobs for those that are considered skilled process designers in onshore locations, but it is going to decrease the available opportunities that are there for low skilled workers offshore.

Impacts on Society

More academic studies have been done and have projected that RPA and other technological advances will help to usher in a new era of more productivity and more efficient methods that will benefit the global labor market. These gains cannot be directly attributed to RPA alone though. Many researchers or associations believe that up to 35% of all jobs are going to be automated by 2035.

At the same time, Professor Willcocks, who is the author of an LSE paper, spoke about an increase in job satisfaction and intellectual stimulation which can be characterized as technology taking technology advances out of humankind. This reference to robots taking over people's daily mundane and repetitive workload leaves them to do something more interesting or meaningful.

RPA and Robotics

As you have seen earlier in this chapter, robotics process automation is going to make it to where robots can automate their tasks so that they do not have to be trained on how to do something each day. This is going to help humans move on to doing something that is more interesting and meaningful, which is going to make the production quality of products being made go up. This will then result in companies putting more focus on customer service and other areas where they may be lacking because they now have the resources to retrain their employees to do another job.

Chapter 5: Mobile Robots

Mobile robots are robots that are capable of locomotion. These robots are typically listed as a subfield to information engineering as well as robotics.

Mobile robots can move throughout their environment and not be stuck in one place. Mobile robots can be autonomous or AMR (autonomous mobile robots). This indicates that they can navigate through an uncontrolled environment without guidance from human or electromechanical devices. On the other hand, mobile robots are going to depend on guidance software that is going to make it so that they can cover a route that has been pre-programmed while in a controlled environment. These types of vehicles are known as autonomous guided vehicles or AGVs. By contrast, factory robots are going to mostly be stationary because they work with a jointed arm and a gripper assembly (they can also work with an end-stage stimulus) that cannot be moved because it is attached to its workspace.

Mobile robots are starting to be more ordinary in factory and commercial settings. Medical centers have begun to use mobile robots that can follow a predetermined route to move product that is too heavy for human workers to move. Warehouses have started to install mobile robotic systems so that the materials from the shelves can be efficiently moved to the fulfillment zones. Current researches, as well as most universities, most often concentrate on mobile robots. The security and military fields also make use of mobile robots. Domestic mobile robots include entertainment robots that can perform household tasks like gardening or vacuuming.

The modules for mobile robots will be the controller, the control programs, actuators, and sensors. The controller is usually going to be a microprocessor that is tied to a distant control or a laptop. The programs will be a scripting language of some sort like C or C++. Sensors will depend on the conditions set for the robot. The conditions could include processing skills, sensors to sense what is being touched, how close they are to something, forming a map based off of its location, or even the avoidance of collisions, and any number of other applications.

Classification

Mobile robots fall under the following classifications:

1. *The environment where they travel*

     a. Arctic robots were invented to navigate across ice and abyss-filled climates.

     b. Robots that are used on land or in the home are usually called Unmanned Ground Vehicles or UGVs. They are typically going to move on tracks or wheels but can also cover the robots that have legs. These robots will consist of two or more legs.

     c. AUVs, autonomous underwater vehicles, are what underwater robots are called.

     d. UAVs, uncrewed aerial vehicles, are what aerial robots are called.

2. *The device they use to move*

a. tracks

b. wheels

c. legs

Robot Navigation

1. *Physical distant or tele-op*: this robot is physically teleoperated and is commanded by the driver by using a switch or other distant control devices. The distant is going to either be plugged into a robot directly or act as an attachment to a laptop or some other means of operation. A tele-op'd robot will be utilized to make sure that the operator is safe. A few examples of distant manual robots are the Robotics Design's Anatroller ARI - 50 and ARI - 100. There is also KumoTek's MK-705 Rosterbot and Foster-Miller's Talon.

2. *Guarded tele-op*: this teleop robot is guarded and can detect and move around obstacles but is going to navigate as it is driven. A manual tele-op robot can be compared to this. There are not many moving robots that present only guarded tele-op (if there are any).

3. *Line-following car*: They would follow a visual line that was embedded on the ceiling or floor or painted. They would also follow an electric wire that was laid out on the floor. Many of these robots function on a basic algorithm that was to "keep the line in the center sensor." These robots wouldn't move around obstacles; instead, they'd stop and wait until whatever was blocking their path was removed. You can still buy line following cars because they are produced by Transbot, FMC, Egemin, HK Systems, and several more. Robots like this are still popular in robotic societies because they are the first step taken when learning about robotics.

4. *Autonomously randomized robot*: autonomous robots that have random motions are going to bounce off walls even if they sense the walls.

5. *Autonomously guided robot*: They have a little bit of data about its destination and the information needed to reach its goal or any places that it will need to stop on its route. Knowledge of where the robot is currently can be determined thanks to at least one of the following methods – sensors, vision, global positioning systems, lasers, and Stereopsis. These location systems will typically use the Monte-Carlo/Markov localization, relative position, and triangulation to figure out exactly where the platform is for the robot to the next goal's path. This robot can collect readings from their sensors that are stamped with both location and time. Take, for example, a PatrolBot. This robot acts as security that sends a notification to the command center when emergencies happen, operates the elevators, and responds to alarms. Other autonomously guided robots can be used in a hospital. Dr. Ahmed Elgammal, a computer scientist, Dr. Simeon Kotchomi, a biologist, and Dr. Qingze Zou, an engineer, helped the artist, Elizabeth Demaray, to create an autonomous robot that has a capability of looking for water and sunlight for a potted plant back in 2013.

Sliding Autonomy

Some of the more capable robots are combined with several stages of navigation under a system that is known as sliding autonomy. Manual mode can be seen to most robots that are guided independently, such as the hospital robot, HelpMate. The Motivity autonomous robot operating system has been used with MapperBot, SpeciMinder, PatrolBot, ADAM, and many other robots that present a range of autonomy that can go from being manually operated to a guarded mode.

History

Time Period	Evolution
1939 - 1945	Due to much advancement in technology in multiple research fields, such as cybernetics and computer science, the first mobile robots were created during World War II. They were mostly flying bombs. Some examples were the V2 and V1 rockets. They have preprogrammed detonations systems and "autopilot". Another is the smart bombs. Using radar control and guiding systems, once near the target, was the only time they would detonate. The current cruise missiles were developed using these robots.
1948 - 1949	'Elsie' and 'Elmer' were built by W. Grey Walter. Both of them were autonomous robots. Since they liked to explore their environment, they were called Machina Speculatrix. Light sensors were installed on the two robots which helped them move when a source of light was located. They could also remove or avoid obstacles that were in their path. These robots proved that simple designs could perform complex behaviors. Two nerve cells could be compared to Elsie and Elmer.
1961 - 1963	'Beast' was created by Johns Hopkins

	University. To move around its surroundings, sonar was installed. Beast could also plug itself in after locating a power socket if its batteries were low.
1969	The robot 'Mowbot' was the first one who could mow a lawn automatically.
1970	A robot with an installed camera was capable of following a white line and was called the Stanford Cart line follower. Calculations were made by the large mainframe that was linked to the robot via radio. The robot 'Shake' was built and researched by the Sanford Research Institute from 1966 to 1972. The jerky motions it displayed made them call it Shakey. This robot featured a radio link, a camera, a rangefinder, and bump sensors. Because of its ability to think before doing its actions, it was acknowledged as the first android. Shake could figure out what needed to be done so that it could complete the task once general commands were provided. A mobile lunar rover by the Soviet Union, Lunokhod 1, explored the moon's surface.
1976	Two uncrewed crafts of NASA's Viking program were sent to Mars.

1980	The public interest in robots rose which resulted in robots being bought to be used in the home. These robots were used for educational or entertainment purposes. Examples would be RB5X (a robot that can still be bought today) as well as the HERO series. The Stanford Card can now move through an obstacle course and make a map of its surroundings.
Early 1980s	The first robot car was built which could reach a speed of 55 mph on an empty street. It was built in Munich's Bundeswehr University by the team led by Ernst Dickmann.
1983	Mihail Sestakov and Stevo Bozinovski controlled a moving robot through a parallel program as a multitasking system of IBM series where only one computer was used.
1986	Gjorgi Gruevski and Stevo Bozinovski used speech commands to control wheeled robots.
1987	The first sensor-based autonomous operation and the cross-country map was demonstrated by the Hughes Research Laboratories.
1988	Mihail Sestakov, Stevo Bozinovski, and Lijana Bozinovska used EEG signals to

	control a mobile robot
1989	BEAM robotics was invented by Mark Tilden.
1990s	The father of the robotic arm, Joseph Engelberger, and his colleagues worked together to design the first commercially available autonomous hospital robot that was produced by Helpmate. The MDARS-1 project was funded by the Department of Defense. The indoor security robot by Cybermotion was the basis of this project.
1991	Used for research activities, an autonomous small mobile robot was developed by Francesco Mondada, Andre Guignard, and Edo Franzi named 'Khepera'. LAMI-EPFL lab supported this project.
1993 - 1994	Used for live volcano exploration, Carnegie Mellon University developed Dante and Dante II.
1994	With guests on board, VITA -2 and VaMP of Ernst Dickmanns of UniBwM and Daimler-Benz drove on Paris' three-lane highway over a thousand kilometers during heavy traffic. 130 km/h was the speed that they have reached. They demonstrated how a mobile robot could

	autonomously drive in free lanes, convoy drive, and change lanes while passing other cars or other cars passing them.
1995	A car was steered by ALVINN, a Semi-autonomous robot, from one coast to the next, under a computer's control for all but 50 miles out of the 2,850 miles. A human controlled the brakes and the throttle.
1995	The programmable mobile robot of Pioneer was available commercially at a cheap price, which allowed for a robotics and university study and research to increase over the next few decades while the university made mobile robotics as their curriculum's vital part.
1996	Cyberclean Systems developed the vacuum cleaning robot that was the first to become fully autonomous. It could self-charge, operate an elevator, and vacuum a hallway without the intervention of a human.
1996 - 1997	Sojourner, a rover carried by the Mars Pathfinder, was sent to Mars by the NASA. The command was sent from Earth to the rover so that it could perform its exploration. A hazard avoidance system was installed on Sojourner which allowed it to explore the unknown terrain

	safely.
1999	Aibo, a robotic dog, was introduced by Sony that could see, walk, and interact with its surroundings. The PackBot was introduced, which was a military robot that could be controlled from a distance.
2001	The Swarm-bots project started. They could be compared to insect colonies. Usually, they are made up of multiple simple robots that can interact together to complete a complex task.
2002	A domestic autonomous mobile robot, Roomba, first appeared that could clean the floor.
2003	Intellibot, a manufacturer of commercial robots, was bought by Axxon Robotics. These robots could clean the floors in office buildings, medical centers, and various other commercial buildings. Floor care robots that were made by Intellibot Robotics LLC were made to operate completely on their own because they were able to map out their surroundings and use various sensors to

	navigate and avoid obstacles.
2004	Mark Tilden made Robosapien commercially available. It was a toy robot.
	The Centibots Project made a hundred autonomous robots. Their goal was to work side by side to map out and search items in an unknown environment.
	A competition of fully autonomous vehicles, DARPA Grand Challenge, first took place in a desert course.
2005	Boston Dynamics created a quadrupled robot. It aimed to carry heavy loads across terrain that was too rough for vehicles to travel.
2006	The production of HelpMate and Aibo was stopped by Sony. The first commercially available robot, TALON-Sword, was released. It featured integrated weapon options and grenade launcher. Asimo by Honda has learned how to climb stairs and run.
2008	A new generation Big Dog's video was released by Boston Dynamics which showed its balance recovery after being kicked to the side and its ability to walk on icy terrain.

2010	The Multi-Autonomous Ground-robotic International Challenge created teams of autonomous vehicles for the goal of mapping, identifying, and tracking humans in a large urban area while avoiding dangerous objects.
2016	A sniper who was wanted for killing five Dallas Texas police officers was killed by the Multi-Function Agile distant-Controlled Robot (MARCbot), which the police used for the first time. Ethical questions were raised due to this incident that referred to the police's use of robots and drones against perpetrators.
Cataglyphis, a rover from the Sample Return Robot Centennial Challenge of NASA, showcased retrieval skills, return capabilities, decision making, sample detection, and autonomous navigation.
2017	The robots for the ARGOS challenge were built to endure working in very difficult situations on oil and gas installations offshore.

Chapter 6: Artificial Intelligence

Artificial intelligence, otherwise known as AI, is often referred to as machine intelligence and it is the intelligence that is commonly shown in machines as opposed to the natural intelligence that is usually seen in humans and various other mammals. When it comes to computer science, artificial intelligence research is going to be listed as a study of intelligence that is shown by devices that can perceive the environment around it in order to take actions that can maximize its chances of being successful in reaching its goals. Informally, the word artificial intelligence will usually be linked to a machine that can copy a human's cognitive function problem-solving or learning.

Definitions often remove how AI has the capability of using intelligence in completing tasks. This is considered to be a phenomenon that is known as the AI effect which can be lead to the quip that is found in Tesler's Theorem that states "AI is whatever hasn't been done yet." Take, for example, special recognition through vision has become known as conventional technology. Modern machines are now capable of things that classify them as AI because they can successfully understand human speech while also competing in high-level strategic games like chess. They can also autonomously operate cars and are intelligent enough to deal with routing in military simulations and content delivery networks.

Artificial intelligence was classified into three different classes by Kaplan and Haenlein, which they borrowed from the management literature – humanized artificial intelligence, human-inspired, and analytical. Analytical artificial intelligence is going to only have characteristics that are consistent with cognitive as well as emotional intelligence when it comes to understanding, as well as recognizing, cognitive elements and human emotions that are factored into the decisions they make. Humanized AI shows characteristics of every competency (emotional, cognitive, emotional, and social intelligence) as well as being self-aware and self-conscious enough to have interaction with others. Human-inspired artificial intelligence must all have human-like appearance besides its perceptive, social, and cognitive abilities. They must be able to clearly communicate with the use of natural language. And the latest advancement called olfaction brings the roots much closer to humans since they can now recognize smells.

Sometime around 1956 was the first foundation of artificial intelligence as an academic discipline. Multiple waves of optimism were experienced in the following years, which have also been followed by many failures and even funding problems. This was named the AI winter, but it was quickly replaced by new AI approaches, triumphs, and more funding given to robotic research. For much of its history, artificial intelligence experimentation has been able to be separated into subfields that typically fail to keep in contact with each other. The subfields can typically be sorted out based on their technical considerations and even a specific set of goals while using particular tools or even analytical differences. These subcategories can also be created based off of social factors that the institution or researchers are interested in.

Artificial research's traditional goals or problems include the ability to manipulate and move objects, natural language processing, perception, learning, representation, planning, knowledge, and reasoning. One of the long-term goals of the field is general intelligence. Approaches include traditional symbolic AI, statistical methods, and computational intelligence. AI uses various tools including mathematical and search optimization, artificial neural networks, and methods that are created because of statistics like economics and probability. The AI field regularly draws on linguistics, philosophy, psychology, information engineering, mathematics, computer science, and so much more.

Artificial intelligence was established on the claim that the intelligence of humans "can be so precisely described that a machine can be made to simulate it." It is because of this philosophical argument that other discussions about the brain and any ethics that are involved in designing androids and other robotics that are provided with the systems needed to have intelligence the same as humans, which produce problems that have been thoroughly explored thanks to myths, philosophy, and fiction ever since antiquity. Some people believe AI is a danger to humanity if the progress is unabated. However, there are others that think AI, unlike other technological revolutions, is going to cause a massive issue when examining unemployment.

In the 21st century, AI technology and methodology have seen a resurgence when it comes to following some of the technology advances that have taken place in computer power, theoretical understanding, and large amounts of data. Artificial intelligence methods have become a vital part of this rapidly advancing industry and have helped to solve multiple problems that are more demanding of their attention in computer science, operations research, and programs engineering.

History

Thought processing androids have been detailed in stories ever since antiquity and have taken up residence in fiction like in *R.U.R* by Karel Capek or *Frankenstein* by Mary Shelley. These characters and their fates have brought about some of the same issues that are now being discussed when it comes to the principles of artificial intelligence.

The study of reasoning for androids first started with theorists and math statisticians. The examination of the logistics of math eventually led to the theory of computation by Alan Turing which would suggest that a machine can copy any plausible act of mathematical deduction through the shuffling of symbols such as 1 and 0. It was this insight that made it to the Church-Turing thesis, where any process of formal reasoning can be simulated by digital computers. Going along with information, cybernetics, and neurobiology's current discoveries, researchers have been led to consider the electronic brain's development a possibility. Turing proposes that "if a human cannot distinguish between responses that come from a machine and a human, then the machine could be considered the intelligent being." The formal design for Turing – complete artificial neurons – was recognized to be the first work in artificial intelligence. It was created in 1943 by McCulloch and Pitts.

The field of artificial intelligence research was first started at a workshop that was taking place at Dartmouth College in 1956. Those that attended were Allen Newell from CMU, John McCarthy from MIT, Herbert Simon from CMU, Arthur Samuel from IBM, and Marvin Minsky from MIT all of which would be considered the leaders and founders of artificial intelligence research. These professors and their students would go on to produce programs that the press would consider to be astounding, and the computers would learn checkers strategies, and by 1959, they were supposedly playing better than humans. They could also solve word problems in algebra, speak English, and prove logical theorems. The Department of Defense of the United States heavily funded researches about AI around the mid-60s. They also established many laboratories around the world. The founders have a very optimistic view of the future of artificial intelligence. As predicted by Herbert Simon, "machines will be capable, within twenty years, of doing any work a man can do." This was agreed by Marvin Minsky who added, "Within a generation... the problem of creating 'artificial intelligence' will be substantially solved."

The difficulties of some of the tasks are what they have failed to recognize; hence, slowing down then progress. Due to the pressure from the US Congress and Sir James Lighthill's criticism, the US and British governments both cut off any artificial intelligence exploratory research. AI winter was what it was known for the next couple of years. This was the time when it was difficult to get funding for a program intended for artificial intelligence.

Due to the expert systems' commercial success, the research for artificial intelligence was brought back in the early 80s. Expert systems are a kind of AI program which focuses on stimulating the analytical and knowledge of the human experts. AI's market hit more than 1 billion dollars in 1985. During this time, the funding for the academic research was restored by the governments of the US and Britain, who became inspired by the Fifth Generation computer project of Japan. However, artificial intelligence once again fell in 1987 due to the Lisp Machine market collapse. This led to the second and longer hiatus of AI.

In the late 90s and early twenty-first century, logistics like medical diagnosis and data mining started using AI. Due to the greater emphasis on solving specific problems and evolvement in AI's computational power, AI's return was a success. This made artificial intelligence closer to other fields. The researchers and their mathematical methods also made a commitment to scientific standards. For the first time in 1997, Garry Kasparov, the reigning world chess champion, was beaten by a computer chess-playing system named Deep Blue.

An exhibition match was made on a quiz show, *Jeopardy*, in 2011 where two of the greatest champions were defeated with a significant difference by IBM's system Watson. Around 2012, improvements to perception and algorithms, faster computers, deep learning, and data-hungry advances began to dominate accuracy benchmarks. The Xbox 360 has a 3D body motion interface which was provided by Kinect. Algorithms that use a lot of AI research were used in Xbox One. Smartphones even have intelligent personal assistants. Four out of five Go matches was won by AlphaGo held on March 2016 against the Go champion. Beating a professional Go player that doesn't have a handicap made him the first Go-playing computer system. The next year, AlphaGo once again won against the number one champion who had been the winner for two consecutive years in the Future of Go Summit. Since Go is more complex than chess, this was a major milestone and finally completed the development of artificial intelligence.

Jack Clark from Bloomberg even said that artificial intelligence had a great year in 2015 due to an increase in the number of programs and projects that focus on or use AI. Also, since 2011, image processing tasks' error rates drastically fell. The increase in neural networks, according to Clark, may be the reason for this drastic change. An increase in research datasets and tools and the rise in cloud computing infrastructures made the neural networks more affordable

A survey in 2017 showed how AI was incorporated in one out of five companies to be used in their processes. The government funding was increased by China in 2016. It resulted in the rapid increase of research output and the huge supply of information which made China a superpower in AI, as believed by observers.

The Basics of AI

AI typically studies its surroundings and takes actions so that their goals are reached. The goal of an AI can be something as simple as winning a game or as complex as doing a mathematical equation. These goals can be induced, or they can be defined explicitly. The goals can be induced implicitly if the AI is programmed for reinforcement learning through a reward system for good behavior and punishments for bad. On the other hand, an evolutionary system can help to induce goals through a fitness function in order to mutate and preferentially replicate a high scoring AI system, which is going to be similar to how animals evolve to achieve goals like finding food or how a dog can be bred through artificial selection because it possesses specific traits. There are some AI systems like the nearest neighbor that will reason through analogy, but these systems are not usually given goals. But to a certain degree, the goals are going to be implicit in their training data. Some systems can be benchmarked should the non-goal system be framed as a system whose goal is to successfully accomplish a narrow classification task.

AI mostly revolves around the use of algorithms. Simpler algorithms can be seen below the more complex algorithms. Simple algorithms are like a game of tic tac toe.

1. If someone poses a threat, then two should be taken in a row, and then the remaining square should be taken; otherwise,

2. should a move "fork" to create two threads at once, that move should be played; otherwise,

3. If the center square is free, it should be taken; otherwise,

4. if your opponent decides to take the corner, you should take the other corner; otherwise,

5. if there is any empty corner, take one; otherwise,

6. any empty square should be taken.

Many AI algorithms can learn from the data that they gather, which can help them enhance themselves by learning new heuristics or help them write other algorithms. There are some learners that you will see described below that include the nearest neighbor, decision trees, and Bayesian networks that could potentially be helpful – should it be given an infinite amount of memory, time, and data to approximate any function, which includes whatever combination of mathematical functions that would best describe the whole world. These learners could move on to know everything by considering each possible hypothesis and then matching it to the data. In practice, it is never possible to consider each possibility thanks to the phenomenon of combinatorial explosion, where the amount of time that is needed to solve a problem ends up growing exponentially. Much AI research includes finding out how to identify and avoid any broad swaths of possibilities that are most likely not going to be useful. Take for instance that you are looking at a map and trying to find the shortest driving route from your hometown to the nearest metropolitan. You can, in most cases, skip going through all of the small towns or anything that is out of the way; which is something that AI would do thanks to a pathfinding algorithm. That way, each route is planned, and you do not have to worry about wasting time getting to your destination.

Problems

One of the overall research goals for artificial intelligence is to create technology that will allow other machines and computers to work in an intelligent manner. The overall problem for this is the simulating of intelligence, which has to be broken down into sub-problems. These will consist of a specific set of traits that are expected by the researchers to display an intelligent system. The traits are described below.

Problem Solving and Reasoning

Algorithms were created by early researchers that showed step-by-step reasoning that humans used whenever they were making a logical deduction or solving puzzles. Sometime in the late 80s and even the early 90s, a new method used in dealing with uncertain and incomplete information was created by the AI researchers. This employed an idea based on economics and probability.

Each of these algorithms was then found to be insufficient when it came to solving large reasoning problems since they were experiencing combinatorial explosions, which meant that they were exponentially slower the bigger the problems grew. In fact, a step-by-step reduction is very rarely used by humans – which early AI researchers were using as a model. Humans usually use intuitive judgments to solve their problems.

Knowledge Representation

Knowledge engineering and knowledge representation are going to be the basis for classic AI research. There are a few expert systems that have attempted to piece together explicit knowledge that is possessed by experts in some narrow domain. On top of that, some projects have tried to gather the commonsense knowledge that is held by an average person piecing it into a database that contains extensive knowledge of the world. Among these things is the comprehensive, commonsense knowledge base that is going to contain properties, categories, objects, and relations that occur between events, times, situations, objects, and states. It also includes cause and effect, knowledge, and many other domains that are not as well researched. A representation of "what exists" is an ontology that sets properties, concepts, relations, and objects together so that a program's agent can interpret them. Their semantics will be captured through individuals, description logic concept, roles, and are usually implemented as properties, individuals, and classes in the Web Ontology Language.

Upper ontology, which is the most general ontology, acts as a mediator between domain ontology to try to provide a foundation to all the other knowledge. Some formal knowledge representations can be used with clinical decision support, content-based indexing and retrieval, and scene interpretation as well as knowledge discovery and many other areas.

Knowledge representation's most difficult problems include:

1. *The qualification problem and the default reasoning*: Many people are aware of working assumptions. Take, for instance, if a bird comes up in your mind while you are talking to someone, then you can usually see a bird in your head and describe it well enough that someone else would know what you are thinking about. However, what you think you know about birds may not be the truth about every bird. In 1969,

John McCarthy identified this problem as a qualification problem: because there is going to be a large number of exceptions to any commonsense rule that AI researchers can represent. Almost nothing is simply marked as true or false in the way that abstract logic actually requires. AI research has to explore every solution to the problem.

2. *The breadth of commonsense knowledge*: the number of atomic facts that a person knows is large. There are research projects that are trying to build a complete knowledge based on commonsense knowledge, but it will require a large amount of laborious ontological engineering which has to be built by hand one concept at a time.

3. *The subsymbolic form of some commonsense knowledge*: what most people know cannot be represented as a fact or a statement that can be expressed verbally. Take, for example, someone who is good at chess. They are going to avoid certain positions because they feel too exposed, or even art critics can look at paintings and know that they are fake. These are subsymbolic institutions, and they are not conscious thoughts. Knowledge of this type provides, supports, and informs a context for conscious knowledge. As with this problem of subsymbolic reasoning, it is hoped that situated AI, statistical AI, or computational intelligence is going to provide a way to represent this type of knowledge.

Planning

Set goals and how they can be achieved is figured out by intelligent planning. The goals must visualize the future. The actions made should match the goals.

When it comes to classical planning problems, one agent is going to assume that it is the system that is acting inside the world by allowing the agents to be certain of the consequences for its actions. However, if the agent is only the actor, then it will require the agent to act without any certainty. This calls for the agent to assess their environments and makes predictions, but also, they must evaluate its predictions and adapt based on these assessments.

Multi-agent planning will use cooperation and competition of multiple agents to reach a specific goal. Emergent behavior is going to be used by swarm intelligence and evolutionary algorithms.

Approaches

There are no established theories that guide the AI research going on. Researchers constantly disagree about many issues. Some long-standing questions that have not been answered is "Should artificial intelligence simulate natural intelligence by studying psychology or neurobiology?" "Or is human biology as irrelevant to AI research as bird biology is to aeronautical engineering?" "Can intelligent behavior be described using simple, elegant principles?" "Or does it necessarily require solving a large number of completely unrelated problems? "

Cybernetics and brain simulation

During the 1940s and 1950s, there were a number of researchers that explored how neurobiology, cybernetics, and information theory tied together. Some of these researchers built machines that would use electronic networks to exhibit rudimentary intelligence, such as W. Grey Walter's turtles or Johns Hopkins Beast. England's Ratio Club and Princeton University's Teleological Society held meetings where many researchers got together. It was not until 1960 that this approach was abandoned, even though, in the 1980s, some elements of it were brought back.

Symbolic

Whenever access to digital computers was made possible, AI began to explore how symbol manipulation could be reduced by human intelligence. CMU, MIT, and Stanford are the center of the research. Good old-fashioned AI, or GOFAI for short, is the name John Haugel gave to these symbolic approaches to AI. It was during the 60s that symbolic approaches started to achieve success when it came to simulating a high-level program in thinking in a small demonstrative program. Approaches are based on cybernetics as well as artificial neural networks that were either pushed into the background or abandoned completely. Research in the 60s and 70s was convinced that symbolic approaches would eventually create a machine with artificial general intelligence and that was thought to be the goal of their field.

Cognitive Simulation

In an attempt to formalize them, Herbert Simon and Allen Newell, both economists, studied the human problem-solving skills. Their work laid the foundation for artificial intelligence along with operations research, management science, and cognitive science. Their research team was using results that they got from psychological experiments in order to develop skills that would help simulate the techniques that people needed to solve problems. This tradition started at CMU and eventually ended up circulating through Soar architecture during the 1980s.

Scruffy or Anti-logic

MIT researchers discovered that ad-hoc solutions are required in solving difficult problems through natural language processing and vision and these researchers argued that any general or simple principles could not capture every aspect of intelligent behavior. Roger Schank was the one to describe the teams' anti-logic approaches using the word scruffy (not neat). Since commonsense knowledge bases have to be built by hand, it became an example of scruffy AI, and this was a complicated concept at one time.

Applications

Any intellectual task can be related to artificial intelligence. The AI effect is a phenomenon wherein you no longer consider a technique to be artificial intelligence if it has become mainstream.

Self-driving cars and drones are just some of the modern AI high profile examples. You can also see them in targeting for online advertisements, judicial decisions, predicting of flight delays, spam filtering, image recognition, online assistants, search engines when games are played like chess or Go, the proving of mathematical theorems, the creation of art, and medical diagnosis.

Social media is slowly taking over TV as a source to reach out to young people, which mean that the big news organizations have to become reliant on social media platforms to get people to read the news. Even major publishers are using artificial intelligence to generate a higher volume of traffic and effectively post more stories.

Healthcare

Findings have suggested that up to 16 billion dollars can be saved if AI is used in diagnosing patients. In 2016, a groundbreaking study in California, with the help of AI, saw the creation of a formula to determine correctly the right dosage of immunosuppressant drugs needed by an organ patient.

Thanks to the doctor's assistance, the healthcare industry has been slowly entered by artificial intelligence. An AI developed by Microsoft has already helped doctors in finding how to treat cancer properly. According to Bloomberg Technology, there has already been a huge number of drugs and research linked to cancer that has been developed. To be more detailed, over 800 vaccines and medicines have been made to treat cancer supposedly. However, this can have a negative effect on doctors since finding the right medication for the patient from too many options can be difficult.

Hanover is an on-going project by Microsoft. Memorizing all the researchers and studies about cancer and helping predict the most effective combination of drugs is the main goal. Fighting myeloid leukemia is a project that is currently being worked on. This type of cancer is fatal, and there has been no improvement in its treatment over the decades. One study has also found that the ability of AI to locate skin cancer can be compared to a trained doctor. Another study has also been conducted where AI is used in finding and monitoring several patients that are at higher risk. The AI asks questions to each patient based on the information collected from live doctor-and-patient interactions.

Surgeons also conducted a study at the National Medical Center for children located in Washington. The team of surgeons used an autonomous robot under their supervision to perform surgery on the bowel of a pig. They observed that the robot did much better than a skilled human doctor. Watson, an AI computer owned by IBM, has also made a diagnosis of a woman suffering from leukemia.

Automotive

Advancements in AI have contributed to the growth of the automotive industry by creating and evolutionizing self-driving vehicles. AI has been used by more than thirty companies in 2016 to create driverless cars. Some of those companies include Apple, Google, and Tesla.

A self-driving car's functions are composed of several components. The systems incorporated on these vehicles include navigation, mapping, braking, collision prevention, and lane changing. When combined, these are going to work off a high-performance computer that is inside of the complex vehicle.

Though still being tested, driverless trucks are now also been created thanks to current improvements in autonomous automobiles. The government of the United Kingdom already passed Legislation on startup testing of self-driving trucks in 2018. A non-self-driving truck is going to be followed by a fleet of self-driving trucks. The Freightliner Inspirations is being tested at the same time by an automobile corporation in Germany called Daimler. This will be a semi-autonomous truck used on the highway.

One of the big factors that influence if a vehicle can be driverless is if the mapping is working properly. In general, maps of the area where a vehicle will be driving are generally pre-programmed. This map is going to include street lights and curb heights so that the vehicle is familiar with the area. However, an algorithm has been already worked on by Google with the aim of eliminating the need for pre-programmed maps and instead will replace it with a device that is going to adjust to the new surroundings that the vehicle goes through.

Some of the already developed self-driving cars don't have breaks or steering wheels. They are a part of a research study focused on the creation of an algorithm that can maintain a safe environment for the passengers through being familiar with driving conditions and speed.

Another factor that is influencing the driverless automobile is how safe the passenger is. In order to make a driverless automobile, engineers have to program it so that it can handle situations that can bring higher risks. These may include head-on pedestrian collisions. They aim to keep both the pedestrian and passenger safe. There is a possibility that the car has to make a decision that is going to place someone in danger. In other words, the car may have to decide to save its passengers or the pedestrian. The program is going to be a crucial part of creating a successful driverless car.

Finance and Economics

Financial institutions have used artificial neural networks for a long time to detect changes or claims that are not inside of the customer's normal spending. These charges are then flagged for human investigation. Since 1987, banking has been using artificial intelligence every time a Fraud Prevention Taskforce is set up by the Security Pacific National Bank so that unauthorized use of credit cards can be countered. Financial services also use AI in programs like Moneystream and Kasisto.

Banks now use AI to manage properties, invest in stocks, maintain the bookkeeping, and organize operations. Whenever a business is not taking place, or any changes have happened overnight, AI can react to it. A simulated financial trading competition took place in 2001 wherein a robot beat a human. It also monitors the user's behavioral patterns; thus, helping reduce financial and fraud crimes.

Video Games

Video games also use artificial intelligence so that NPCs (non-player characters) can have dynamic, purposeful behavior. On top of that, pathfinding also uses AI techniques. Some studies think NPCs in video games can solve problems for production tasks.

Military

In 2015, militaries around the world had been spending money amounting to $7.5 billion on robotics from $5.1 billion. Military drones have become a useful asset because of the autonomous actions that they present the military. Vladimir Putin said in 2017 that, "whoever becomes the leader in artificial intelligence will become the ruler of the world." Many AI researchers are keeping themselves from AI's military applications.

Chapter 7: Machine Learning

'Machine learning' refers to the subfield found in PC (Personal Computer) science where PCs are given the tools needed to learn without being programmed by a person.

The evolution of this study included pattern recognition and learning theory that can be found in the artificial intelligence field. The machines are going to explore the study and learn how to construct algorithms and make predictions with the data that is provided for these algorithms like overcoming the static programming instructions. These instructions are going to be driven by data for predictions or decisions by using basic inputs of data to build a model.

Algorithms are invented in computing tasks and carried out with optimum performance. This is where you typically employ machine learning. An example of this is the sorting that your email does in an effort to keep your email secure.

Machine learning tends to overlap with PC statistics where predictions are made through a PC that has strong ties to optimize mathematical equations. This also makes it to where theories, methods, and applications dominate the field.

Data mining, which uses data analysis, is often confused with machine learning. Unsupervised learning is what you also call data analysis. Even if it is unsupervised, machine learning should also learn to create a baseline for its behavior before finding meaningful anomalies.

In the data analytic field, machine learning is going to be used to create methods that are complex along with algorithms that are going to be used in predictions. These predictions are known as predictive analytics when used commercially. The predictions are going to enable researchers, analysts, engineers, and data scientists to make reliable decisions as a way to uncover any insights that may be hidden by learning from data trends and historical relationships.

Back in 2016, machine learning was made a buzzword for the Gartner hype cycle while it was at the peak of its inflated expectations. Due to the fact that finding patterns is difficult, there is often not enough training to go around.

Tasks and Problems

Depending on the learning's nature, you can classify machine learning into three categories:

1. *Unsupervised learning*: labels are not going to be given for the learning algorithms that are used which are going to leave it to find its own structure in the input. You can use unsupervised learning as a goal in finding patterns that are hidden in the data that you are using or as a means to an end.

2. *Supervised learning*: your PC is going to be given inputs as well as the outcome that you are going to want so that the PC can learn a general rule in how to map out the input and outcomes.

3. *Reinforcement learning*: there is going to be a PC program that works with a dynamic environment to perform specific goals such as when you play a game against an opponent. Feedback will be given to you by the program in terms of rewards and punishments as it navigates the space of the problem.

There is semi-supervised learning that is going to fall between supervised and unsupervised. This is going to be when you are going to give training signals that are not complete with the training set so that the program has to do some of the work.

Transduction is going to be whenever the principle takes on the entire problem such as learning times. But this is not going to work whenever targets are missing.

Machine learning also includes categories such as learning, where the program is going to learn the inductive bias of the program based on experiences that have happened before.

Developmental learning is going to be the same as robot learning where the program is going to be able to generate its own sequence from the learning situations that it is put through so that it can learn novel skills by interactions with humans and other programs and self-exploration.

Yet another category of machine learning is going to happen when you consider what the outcome is from the machine learning system:

1. The classification of inputs is going to be divided into at least two classes where the user is going to have to produce a model that is going to take the inputs that are not seen by the user from these classes. This is going to usually happen in supervised learning, such as when your email filters between spam and not spam.

2. Reversion is also going to be supervised for the outcomes to be continuous instead of being discrete.

3. Clustering is going to take the input sets and divide them into various groups. However, the difference between clustering and classification is that the groups are not going to be known to the user before they are made, which makes this an unsupervised task.

4. Density estimation is going to locate the distribution for the inputs in that space.

5. Dimensionality reduction takes the input and simplifies it so they can be mapped to the lowest dimension.

6. Topic modeling will take a problem from the program that is inserted by a user and tasked to see if the documents that were inserted cover related topics.

A classification machine learning model is going to be able to be validated by a technique that uses accuracy estimation such as a holdout. A holdout is going to split the data when training and testing your set before evaluating the test set on the model's performance. However, if you look at n fold cross-validation, then you are going to see that the data will randomly be split into subsets where the k-1 instances are going to be used in training the model while the k-instance is going to be used in testing the predictive ability for the training model that you are using.

Along with this, the holdout and the cross-validation method is going to use samples for the instances where the replacement comes from the dataset and how it is going to be able to be used in assessing the model's accuracy.

On top of that, there is an overall accuracy that an investigator finds; it is going to be reported for specificity and sensitivity, such as the true negative rate and the true positive rate – which means that the true negative and true positive rates are sometimes going to report false positive rates or false negative rates.

However, it is these rates that are going to fail to show the numerator and denominator for the equation. Your total operating characteristic is going to be an effective method that is going to show the model's diagnostic abilities. Total operating characteristic will also reveal the numerators and denominators that were mentioned previously in the rates, which will mean that the total operating characteristic is going to show you more information than you were able to use with the receiver operating characteristic, which is going to fall under the area under the curve.

Due to what it is, machine learning often brings up many ethical questions. The systems that are trained to work with the data that you collect are going to be biased based on the exhibits that the biases are going to be used on, which is going to digitalize the cultural prejudices. Therefore, the responsibility that comes from collecting data is going to be a big part of machine learning.

Due to the language that you use when dealing with machine learning, you are going to be using machines that are trained on a bias.

Neural networks and deep learning

Neural networks are going to be programming paradigms that are biologically inspired to enable a PC to learn from data that is observed.

Deep learning is a set of techniques that you are going to use for neural networks.

Both neural networks and deep learning is going to give you the best solution to any problem that you may come up against when you are working with image, speech, and natural language recognition and processing.

The human visual system is complex and one of the most interesting things that you can study because you are never going to fully understand how it works with the other parts of your body.

Take handwriting, for instance, many people are going to be able to look at something that is written and be able to tell you what is written without any problem, but the little effort that it takes to recognize what is written is actually deceptive. If you look at the different hemispheres of your brain, you are going to realize that your visual cortex has several millions of neurons that are going to be connected. However, your vision is not going to be connected to your visual cortex, but instead, a series of cortices that involve your vision; therefore, making it to where you can process even the most complex of images.

The inside of your head is essentially a super PC that has been fined tuned by evolution. The ability to recognize handwriting is not always easy, but your brain has adapted to where you will do it unconsciously. It is not very often that we take the time to think of how complex our visual system truly is.

Just like it is difficult to recognize visual patterns, a PC is not going to have these issues. However, it is going to be different than how we do it ourselves. Our brains recognize shapes and how things are written out, but how do you tell a PC this? You are going to have to make out rules, and those rules are going to end up getting lost in the exceptions and caveats that you are going to have to create.

The neural network approach is going to look at the problem in a different way though. It is going to take a large number of numbers that are handwritten and be trained to recognize the various shapes so that it can do what our brain can do. Essentially, the neural network is going to use the examples that are inside of the data you input to infer to rules that are set in place as their way to recognize handwritten numbers. The more you add to the number of examples that train the program, the more the network is going to be able to learn more handwriting options to improve its accuracy.

Neural networks are going to work with an artificial neuron that is known as a perceptron, which was developed in the 60s by Frank Rosenblatt. But when we look at it today, it is going to be used like other models of artificial neurons. Your main neuron is going to be known as the sigmoid neuron. To understand the sigmoid neuron, you have to understand the perceptrons.

Perceptrons are going to take several binary inputs and give you a single binary outcome. Rosenblatt came up with a single rule that will be used when dealing with the outcome of perceptrons. This is where weights came in as a way to express the real number, and they bring importance to the inputs and outcomes. The outcome for the neuron is going to either be zero or one and determine the weight of the sum and if it is less than or greater than the threshold value.

Your threshold value is going to be a real number that is going to be used in the parameters for the neuron. Think of the perceptron as a device that is going to make its decisions by weighing the evidence.

For example, if you want to go on a family outing, there are several things that you are going to have to look at to determine if you are going to be able to go on the outing as planned:

1. Is the car big enough for everyone that wants to go?

2. Is the weather going to be good?

3. What do you need to pack for the amount of time that you are going to be out?

Each factor is going to be able to be represented by a binary variable. By looking at the weights and the threshold for your problem, you can create different models for the decision-making process. Your perceptron is going to be what decides if you go on your outing or not. When you drop the threshold, you are going to most likely go on your outing with your family.

Keep in mind that your perceptron is not going to be a complete model of the decision-making process that a human can do. However, your perceptron is going to be able to weigh different evidence to make the decisions that you need to make, which should seem more plausible for a complex network of perceptrons that are going to make small decisions that you may not notice are being made.

While a learning algorithm sounds like the way to go, how are you going to create an algorithm for a neural network? Think about if you have a network for your perceptrons that you can use to solve problems. The inputs for the network are going to be like the raw pixel data that is scanned into the program so that the network can learn weights and biases for the outcome to be classified correctly. If you make any changes to the weight in the network, your outcome is going to correspond with the change that you made.

However, the reality of perceptrons is that when a change is made to the weights, then there is the possibility that the perceptron is going to flip completely due to that change. This change is going to cause the behavior of your entire network to change completely into a more complex behavior. So, while one of your numbers is going to be classified correctly, your network is going to be behaving in a way that is going to be hard to control.

Your network's new behavior is going to make it difficult to see how your weights and bases need to be modified so that your network is closer to the behavior that you want. Therefore, there must be a clever way of getting around this issue that may not be obvious instantly.

You can overcome the problem just by bringing in a new neuron known as the sigmoid neuron. These neurons are going to be like perceptrons, but they are going to be modified so that when you make small changes, they are only going to give you a small change in your outcome rather than chancing that your outcome changes completely. This is vitally important, and the sigmoid neuron is going to be enabled to learn the behavior of the network.

Your sigmoid neuron is going to have inputs that are similar to your perceptron. However, it is going to be able to take any value that falls between zero and one, which means that you can use the decimal points that fall between these two numbers as a valid input for your sigmoid neuron. Just like a perceptron, your sigmoid is going to have a weight for every input as well as a bias that covers everything in that neuron. However, your outcome is not going to be zero or one; it is going to be known as a sigmoid expression, and it is going to be defined by this equation:

σ(z)≡1/1+e−z

Another way to look at it is to put the outcomes of your sigmoid neuron with your inputs:

1/1+exp(−∑jwjxj−b)

When you first look at your sigmoid neuron, they are going to look very different than your perceptrons. However, the algebraic expression for the sigmoid expression is going to seem opaque and like you are never going to be able to master it. However, you are going to be able to because there are many similarities between your perceptrons and your sigmoid neurons.

In an effort to understand the similarities, you need to look at a perceptron model like $z \equiv w \cdot x + b$ where you have a large positive number. Which then means $e^{-z} \approx 0$ $e^{-z} \approx 0$ and $\sigma(z) \approx 1$ are equal. Ultimately, your sigmoid neuron is going to be a large positive number just like it would be for the perceptron.

Now, think of it as if you were working with negative numbers, then your sigmoid behavior will be the same as the perceptron. The only time you are going to see the deviation from your perceptron model is of modest size.

But what is your mathematical form of σ? The truth of the matter is that the exact form for this variable is not to impact because we are going to want to focus on the shape of our expression.

Should this function be a step expression, then your sigmoid neuron is going to end up being a perceptron due to the fact that the outcome would be either zero or one depending on if your equation gives you a positive or negative outcome.

When you use the function for σ, then you are going to get a perceptron that is smooth. How smooth your expression is, though, is not something you need to spend much time focusing on. The smoothness is simply going to modify the weights and bias which is then going to change the outcome for your sigmoid neuron.

Thanks to calculus, your outcome is going to be predicted by this equation:

$\Delta \text{outcome} \approx \sum_j \partial \text{outcome} / \partial w_j \Delta w_j + \partial \text{outcome} / \partial b \, \Delta b,$

Your sum that is found over all of your weights and your outcome is going to show a partial derivative for your outcome with the respect that is needed for your weights. You should not get too worried if you find that you are not comfortable working with partial derivatives. Your expression above is going to look complex due to all of the partial derivatives that are in it, but you are actually going to see that it is fairly simple by looking at your outcome as a linear expression. The linearity is going to be easy to pick out smaller changes that are done to the weights and bases to get to the change that you want in your outcome. Therefore, your sigmoid neuron is going to have the same behavior as the perceptron, which is going to make it to where it is easier for you to figure out how to change your weights and biases to change the outcome.

If the shape is what matters most, then it is not going to be an exact form which is going to be the reason for the use of the o in the equation. When you are looking at the changes that cause you to use a different activation expression, then the value for that partial derivative is going to change in the equation. So, when you compute those derivatives later, your function is going to take the algebra and simplify it so that the exponentials have properties that you can work with when differentiated.

As you interpret your outcome that comes from the sigmoid neuron, you are going to see that one of the biggest differences is going to be the perceptrons and the neurons where the neurons do not result in zero or one. They can have any outcome as long as the outcome is a real number and it falls between zero and one. This is going to be useful when you want your outcome to represent the average intensity for the pixels that are in an image. However, sometimes this is going to be a problem.

Take, for instance, if you want your outcome to say that your image is nine or is not nine. It is going to be easier to do this in the event that your outcome is zero or one for your perceptron. However, in practice, you are going to have to set up a convention to deal with this so that you can interpret the outcome for at least half of the image which is going to indicate the number you want it actually to be. This means that any outcome that is less than half means that the outcome is not going to be what you want it to be.

Big Data

It seemed that 2012 was the year that the big data technologies came around and were everything to everyone. But in 2013 big data analytics became a thing. When you get a hold of substantial amounts of data, you are going to have to manage it, but you are also going to want to pull out the most useful information from the collections, and this is going to be a more difficult challenge. Big data is not only going to change the tools that you use, but it is also going to change the way that people think about the extraction and interpretation of data.

Usually, data science is going to be trial and error, which is going to be impossible whenever working with datasets that are larger and heterogeneous. However, the more data that is available, there are usually going to be fewer options that are going to be constructed for the predictive models due to the fact that there are not going to be many tools that are capable of processing a huge amount of information in a reasonable amount of time. Also, the traditional statistical solutions are going to focus on the analytics that is static, which is going to limit the analysis samples that are frozen in time and are typically going to give you results that are surpassed and unreliable.

However, other alternatives are going to fix the problems that you have about research domains that are going to be expanded, and this is going to be machine learning. Statistics and PC science have applications coming out that are going to focus on the development of algorithms that are going to be fast and efficient for processing data in real time with the goal being to deliver predictions that are accurate.

Some applications are going to be used in business cases, such as telling them how much product they should buy or to detect fraud. The techniques used in machine learning also solve application problems like figuring out statistics in real time as well as giving a reliable analysis by using generic and automatic methods to simplify the data scientist tasks.

Machine Learning and Reversions

When looking at statistical modeling, you will notice that reversion analysis is going to be the process of estimating the various relationships you see between variables. This is going to include the techniques that you use when analyzing and modeling several variables at once whenever you are focused on showing the relationship between an independent and dependent variable.

Reversion analysis is going to assist you in understanding how the usual value for the dependent variable is going to change while the independent variable is not going to change. Reversion is also going to estimate the conditional expectation for the variable that is dependent based on the independent variable and the average value for that variable.

Less commonly, you are going to see the quantile or the location parameters for the conditional distribution of the variable that is dependent based on what the independent variable is. In most cases, your estimate is going to be an expression for the independent variable, which is going to be called the reversion expression. When dealing with reversion analysis, you are also going to be showing your interest in the characterization of the variation for the dependent variable against the expression which will be described as the probability distribution.

One approach that you can take is a conditional analysis which is going to take the estimate for the maximum instead of the average of the dependent variables based on the independent variable that is given so that you can decide if the independent variable is necessary but not sufficient for the value that is given to the dependent variable.

You are going to use reversion for forecasting and when it overlaps with machine learning. You will also use it as a way to understand the relationship between the independent and dependent variables. When dealing with a restricted circumstance, you can use reversion to infer the causal relationship between the variables. However, this can end up giving you a false relationship; therefore, you need to be cautious in using reversion.

There are some techniques that you can use for reversion like linear reversion or least squares reversion. Your reversion expression is going to be defined in terms of finite numbers which are not going to have a known parameter. Nonparametric reversion is going to be the technique that is used when allowing the reversion expression to be used for a set of expressions which may cause infinite dimensional.

Your reversion analysis performance is going to be the methods that you practice as a form of data generating processes and how it ties into the reversion approach that you use – being that the true form of data generating is not always going to be known since reversion analysis will then depend on the extent of the assumptions that you are making.

Your assumptions need to be testable to see if there is a sufficient amount of data being provided.

Machine Learning and Robotics

Now that you know what machine learning is, it shouldn't surprise you that this term has heated up interest in robotics and has not altered much over the past years. But how does machine learning relate to robots?

Robotics has only a few developments currently that led to other developments, including machine learning.

Here are five current machine learning applications that can be seen in robotics:

1. *Computer vision*: there are some that would say that robot vision or machine vision is the correct term because 'robot seeing' is going to involve more than computer algorithms. Roboticists and engineers have studied what type of camera hardware will allow a robot to process the physical data around them. Robot vision and machine vision is closely linked. They can be credited to the creation of automatic inspection systems and robot guidance. The two only has a small difference in kinematics that is applied to robot vision, which will encompass the comment frame calibration and the robot's ability to affect its environment physically.

   An influx in big data has helped to push forward the advances of computer vision, which has further helped machine learning based on structured prediction learning techniques at many universities.

2. *Imitation learning*: imitation learning is closely related to observational learning which is a behavior that can be seen in infants and toddlers. Imitation learning is considered an umbrella category for reinforcement learning or the challenge of getting an agent to act in the world to maximize its rewards. This approach has common features, namely probabilistic models and Bayesian. The question, in the end, is whether imitation learning is going to be able to be used for humanoid robots.

   An important part of robotics, imitation learning has characteristics of mobility outside of factory settings in domains such as search and rescue and construction, making it challenging to program robotic solutions manually.

3. *Self-Supervised learning*: generating their own training examples will be allowed to robots because of self-supervised learning approaches so that they can improve their performances. This is going to include priority training as well as data captured close range that is going to be used to

translate ambiguous sensor data that is long range. Robots with optical devices have this installed on them so they can reject and detect objects.

Cornell and Stanford created a solid example called Watch-Bot that uses a laptop and laser pointer, 3D sensor, and a camera to find normal human activities, which are patterns that are going to be learned through methods of probability. To target a reminder, a laser pointer is used by Watch-Bot in objects. In a test, humans are reminded by the bot almost 60% of the time, but the robot has no concept of what it is doing or why it is doing it.

4. *Medical and assistive technologies*: an assistive robot is a device that can sense and process sensory information before performing an action that is going to end up benefiting a person with disabilities and seniors. These movement therapy robots will provide a therapeutic and diagnostic benefit. Since they are still cost-prohibitive for hospitals abroad and in the United States, they are still not being out in the lab.

Some of the early examples of assistive technologies are a desktop vocational assistant robot or the DeVAR. It was Stanford and Palo Alto Veterans Affairs Rehabilitation Research and Development who developed DeVAR in the early 1990s. There are still studies done on machine learning-based robotic assistive technologies. The MICO robotic arm is one example. It is an assistive machine with an autonomy that uses a Kinect sensor to observe the world. These implications are going to be more complex, but they are going to provide the world with smarter assistive robots that can adapt better to the needs of the user.

The advancement in machine learning can also be seen in the medical world. Though medical facilities don't use it yet, robotics has been advancing at a rapid pace.

5. *Multi-Agent learning*: multi-agent learning has some key components, namely negotiation and coordination, which will involve robots based on machine learning that are created with the goal of finding equilibrium strategies and adapting to a robot's shifting landscape. For example, no-regret learning tools, which involve weighted algorithm, are included in multi-agent learning approaches that are going to help boost the learning outcomes that are tied into the multi-agent learning and planning that is found in distributed control systems that are market-based.

In late 2014, a more solid example of an algorithm that is being used for distributed robots or agents was made in the lab of MIT for decision and information systems. Robots were able to collaborate to build a more inclusive and better learning model that was done by a single robot with the basis of building exploration and the way that the rooms are laid out while autonomously building a knowledge base.

Catalogs are made by every robot which they then combine to the datasets of other robots, where the standard algorithm is outperformed by the distributed algorithm when making this sort of knowledge base. This sort of machine learning approach, while this is not a perfect system, is going to allow robots to compare catalogs and reinforce mutual observations while correcting any omissions or overgeneralizations, which will play a role in multiple robotic applications in the near future.

What the Future Holds

As you saw above, machine learning-based approaches in robotics are starting to be combined with challenges and contracts that are put out by military innovators or sponsors that are working for major robotics manufacturers or even startups, while an increase in investments is being seen by auto manufacturers on the next generation of autonomous vehicles.

Because of what machine learning can do, it is being used to help further advance robotics and make robots more complex when it comes to dealing with data and how they interpret this data.

Chapter 8: Autonomous Vehicles

Self-driving cars are also known as robot cars or autonomous cars or even driverless cars. They are vehicles that will sense the environment they are in and move without human input or very little human input.

Autonomous cars are going to come with a variety of sensors that will help them to evaluate their surroundings like initial measurement units, GPS, odometry, sonar, computer vision, Lidar, and radar. There are also advanced control systems that will interpret the sensory information to identify the proper navigation path and any obstacles or signs that may be in the car's path.

Some benefits are going to include increased safety and reduced cost. They will also increase mobility, reduce crime, and increase customer satisfaction. Safety benefits are also going to include a reduction in collisions and injuries that are going to lead to costs because of these collisions. Increase in traffic flow is predicted because of automated cars while also providing enhanced mobility for the poor, elderly, disabled, and children. They are going to make travel easier because drivers are not going to have to drive and navigate the entire time while also lowering their fuel consumption, as well as the need for a parking space.

Some problems that are coming up with self-driving cars are safety, liability, and technology. Whenever someone is in the car, they are going to have a desire to control the vehicle. Not only that, but there are legal frameworks and government regulations that researchers have to go through. Then, it is going to make people feel like they have lost their privacy, which will then lead to security concerns like hackers or terrorism. Add on top of that, people losing their jobs because there is no longer a need for a driver to be behind the wheel. It will also cause an increase in suburbanization travel because it is going to be more convenient.

Semi-Automated Vehicles

The level of automation is one of the basis of many vehicles. They may be classified as fully autonomous or fully manually—driven vehicles.. Semi-automated vehicles are what they are known as. It will take some time before the technology and infrastructure are fully developed for a fully automated vehicle, but while this is being researched, vehicles will increase based on their level of automation. Semi-automated vehicles are going to have an advantage over fully automated vehicles because the driver is still in control of the vehicle.

Fields of Application

Automated Trucks

Many companies are doing testing of automated technology in semi-trucks. In 2016, Uber bought a self-driving trucking company, Otto, wherein they had to demonstrate their trucks on the highway before Uber bought them. Then, in 2017, a San Francisco-based startup announced that they were going to be partnering with a truck manufacturer by the name of Peterbilt so that they can deploy and test automated technology in the Peterbilt vehicles. Waymo is supposedly doing testing of automated technology in trucks, but the project has no provided timeline.

Also, in 2018, San Francisco-based Starsky Robotics completed a driverless trip to Florida for seven miles. This made them the first player in the game of a driverless truck on a public road.

Over in Europe, truck platooning is starting to be considered with the Safe Road trains for the Environment approach.

Lockheed Martin along with funding that is coming from the United States Military has developed an automated truck conveying system that is going to place a truck in the lead that is run by a human and then there are going to be trucks that follow it autonomously. This is being developed as part of the Army's Autonomous Mobility Applique System (AMAS). In 2014, this system consisted of an automated driving package that will be installed in up to nine different types of vehicles that will have to go through at speeds of 40 mph over driving for 55,000 hours. In 2017, AMAS was starting the plans to field up to 200 trucks that are part of a rapid fielding program.

Transport Systems

Transport systems that are created for automated cars are starting to be operated in cities, such as parts of the UK, France, Italy, and Belgium, and in the Netherlands, Spain, and Germany, they are publically testing them in traffic. The UK launched a public trial for an automated pod, LUTZ Pathfinder, located in Milton Keynes. PSA Peugeot- Citroen has been allowed to run trials in Paris by the government of France on the summer of 2014. The experiments were planned to move on by 2016 to cities like Strasbourg and Bordeaux. The alliance that is between the companies from France, Valeo and THALES, has been allowing for tests of their own to be run. Over in New Zealand, using automated vehicles for public transportation have been already planned in cities such as Tauranga and Christchurch.

Then, in China, an automated minibus has been produced which can seat 14 people without a driving seat. There have been over 100 vehicles produced, and 2018 marked the first year for a commercial automated service available in China. These mini-buses should move on to level four, and this is going to be a driverless environment on a closed road.

Chapter 9: Speech Recognition

Speech recognition is an interdisciplinary subfield that falls under computational linguistics, which will be used in the development of methodologies and techniques that will help machines to recognize and translate spoken language into text. This is also known as computer speech recognition, speech to text (STT), or automatic speech recognition (ASR). Speech recognition will incorporate the knowledge and research needed for computer science, linguistics, and electrical engineering.

Some systems will require training to take place where the speaker is going to read the vocabulary or text into the system. The voice of the person will then be analyzed by the system and be used in fine-tuning the recognition of the speech of that person, which will help increase accuracy. A speaker dependent system uses training while a speaker independent system does not require training.

Speech recognition applications will include things like voice dialing, call routing, simple data entry, the determining of the speaker's characteristics, aircraft, speech to text processing, preparation of structured documents, and domotic appliance control search.

The term voice recognition refers to the identification of the speaker instead of what they are saying. By recognizing the speaker, the task of translation in systems is going to be simplified.

When you look at speech recognition from a technological perspective, it has a long history with multiple waves of innovations. One of the most recent waves is thanks to big data and deep learning. These advances not only can be seen due to the surge of academic papers that have been published but also by the worldwide industry adoption with the different deep learning methods that have been used when it comes to designing and deploying these speech recognition systems. You can see this innovation in companies like SoundHound, Microsoft, IBM, Amazon, and Apple.

Speech Recognition in Robotics

Have you ever seen a robot speak? This is possible thanks to speech recognition!

As we mentioned earlier, speech recognition will be classified into two different categories: Speaker independent and Speaker dependent.

Systems that are *speaker dependent* will be trained by one person, and that person is going to be the one who is using the system. These systems are efficient and can get a high command count; however, the system will only give responses to the person that has trained the system.

Speaker independent systems will be trained to respond to words of an individual who speaks. The voice input device will be mounted on a controller; therefore, the commands being given related to movement are going to be given by voice and then converted into digital form. This is going to be done by an analog to digital converter. The commands will be inputted into a microphone, and then electrical signals can change the voice into the movements. Once these digital signals are given to the robotic controller, then the filtering device will be used to take the data in the form of voice. To improve accuracy and voice, there will be a conversion modeling process that will form a system response.

System Recognition Circuit

To train the circuit of up to 40 words, you will think about it like this. You will be pressing 1 in order to train the system in that first word. By pressing any number, a red LED is going to go out. These numbers will then be displayed on a digital display. Once you press the pound button, it will train the system. By pressing the pound button, it will be sending signals to a chip that is going to listen to training words and will then turn the LED on. To do a test, the next step will be to say the word that you want the system to recognize; this will be when the microphone is used. Once the word is accepted, the LED is going to blink. You will do this for all 40 words, and you should see each word entered on the display.

Speech recognition systems can be broken down into four distinct parts:

1. Speech recognition will be using the separated audio.
2. Linear separation of sources.
3. Computation of missing features from an output which is going to be after it has been filtered.
4. Multiple channels after it have been filtered.

Once the machine has filtered the speech, the robot will carry out the command that is being asked. As technology advances, robots will be able to use speech recognition programs not only to take commands but also to communicate with humans and even other robots when it comes to completing tasks.

Chapter 10: Drones

UAV or uncrewed aerial vehicles are commonly called drones, which are aircraft that do not require human piloting. UAVs are part of the uncrewed aircraft systems which can include UAVs that are controlled from the ground or a system of communications that happens between the two. The way that the UAV flies may operate based off of various degrees of autonomy, which is either going to be controlled from a distant control or autonomously through an onboard computer.

Drones were originally used for missions that were too dangerous or dirty for humans, and they were mostly used in military applications, but their use quickly spread to commercial, recreational, scientific, agricultural, and other applications, such as surveillance, product delivery, policing, peacekeeping, photography, smuggling, and racing.

Drones and Robotics

Onboard Computers

The next generation of drones and robots will be smarter, faster, and lighter than those that came before them. This is only possible thanks to the streamlined solutions that are going to combine several computing functions into a single board. Qualcomm drones and robotic technology is going to make it possible to reduce the onboard computer footprint while still presenting a strong connection, long battery life, and advanced processing power. With a smaller footprint, there is going to be less complexity to the design, which means that drones will be more affordable for a wider audience.

Single Board Technology

With sleeker engineering, the drones are going to be lighter and easier to use thanks to Snapdragon Flight. This technology will integrate 4K high-resolution camera support along with a highly accurate location positioning and even real-time flight controls which will all be mounted on a single board; thus, enabling the OEMs to be smaller and more robust.

Heterogeneous Platform

Building smart drones and robotic components with a heterogeneous platform will help OEMs create safer and lighter drones and robots that will ultimately reduce the cost of the robot, which is going to open it up to more consumers.

Autonomous Flight

OEMs can be made to be self-aware and autonomous thanks to the advancements that have been made in technology. Because of the advanced technology platform, it will combine sensors that are built in with 3D environment mapping, which will allow the drone to fly on its own.

Low Power

By combining several components on a single board, the board is going to provide low power and lightweight solution that will help to present advanced flight connectivity and controls.

Reliable Programs

The Snapdragon Navigator programs will provide intelligent navigation by allowing drones to see and react to objects that may be in their path as they are flying, which is going to provide safer and more reliable navigation.

Intelligent Motor Controller

Snapdragon flight will include intelligent motor control as well as a 500Hz latitude processing that will make the flight experience more stable while increasing battery life and reducing the strain that is placed on the engine.

Position Control

Because of the advanced position control, the flights are smoother than they have been and this will work by combining the GPS, sonar sensors, inertial measurement unit, as well as a barometer sensor which is going to help in supporting enhanced air stability.

Bi-Directional Detection

To avoid collisions and flight path obstacles, bi-directional detection will be used along with the assistance of an electronic speed controller that will recognize any propeller obstructions and even provide flights that can be both indoors and outdoors.

Advanced Wi-Fi

Snapdragon flight uses an 801 process that will support highly advanced Wi-Fi to allow the drone to know exactly where it is, which is going to be helpful when it is being used for police or military matters.

Real-World Application

Drones have become helpful because they can be sent into situations where humans should not be going because it is too dangerous or too dirty. Here are some real-world applications in which drones are being used:

1. *Warfare*: drones first started out in the military and are still being used today. The military has the most cutting-edge features to date and use drones in wartime for surveillance to gather intel without anyone knowing about it. Drones are also used for airstrikes.

2. *Policing*: it is a possibility that you will be tasered from above before too long if you get into an altercation with the police. Police in North Dakota use drones to taser culprits as well as deploy tear gas in the state's effort to crack down harder on crime.

3. *Firefighting*: while this may give you images of drones dropping water onto brushfires, you're a little bit off. Drones are being used to drop fire into the brushfire. This is called controlled burning and is meant to stop the wildfire from spreading further by burning off bushes that they could feed off of. This is also used to maintain biodiversity.

    Back in 2007, drones were being used to help with the Southern California wildfires. Drones would use sensor technology to search through the smoke and figure out how big the blaze was.

4. *Newsgathering machine*: multiple news agencies have brought in drones to be their "eye in the sky".

5. *Oil exploration*: many big oil and gas companies are fully supportive of the use of drones in search for new oil deposits. Right now, the only places that this kind of aircraft is cleared to be operated in this manner are some of the most distant places known to the United States.

6. *Selfie bot*: this one is aimed more for the millennials than anyone else. There is not one technology trend that the millennials will not adopt when it comes to their obsession with selfies. With this one, you will strap the camera onto the

drone and let it fly around whatever event that you are attending.

Even Amazon has found a way to get in on the drone game by making deliveries with drones.

As technology continues to advance, it is likely that we are going to start to see drones play a larger role in air refueling processes, rescue missions, and even as distant tour guides.

Chapter 11: Robotics in Business

Robotics plays a very important role in business. Now, this may make you think of a science fiction future; however, there is a lot of business in a wide array of industries that are turning to robots to complete a task that is too dangerous, laborious, or time-consuming for a human to do.

Factory Manufacturing

A common task for robots to perform is on the product assembly line in a factory space. Manufacturing robots handle tasks like welding, sorting, assembling, and pack and place operation with more efficiency and greater speed than a human. This strength to weight ratio of the electric motors is going to make these robots reliable for tasks that require agility, strength, and consistency. Factory robots reduce the risk of workplace accidents and ensure more control over the product's quality. They can also work in environments that are not safe for a human.

Marketing

Technology companies have come up with robots to demonstrate new inventions while creating a sense of innovation and progress.

These robots are part of an interactive display that can be seen at trade shows where they are sent to compete with traditional marketing tools to catch merchandise and bring them to an employee who is going to enter the request into an automated system. These robots not only save time but reduce errors that can be caused because of inconsistencies in inventory tracking.

Entertainment

The last class of robots that are used in business are those that are meant to entertain people. Robots and robotic displays will be seen in storefronts, theme parks, and on television. These robots are crafted to resemble a real person while others are meant to represent fantastical creatures or mechanical robots from a fictional world. These characters populate science fiction narratives while these special effects robots enter hazardous conditions that are not safe for humans or animals.

Robots Taking Over Jobs

In 2017, it was estimated that a third of US jobs were at high risk of being automated by 2030, which is a higher percentage than those in Britain, Japan, and Germany.

This analysis came from an accounting and consulting firm that said that it is based on the direction and pace of technological progress and the anticipated capabilities of artificial intelligence and robotics.

It is estimated that at least 38% of jobs are going to be at risk for automation in the United States. It is because more US jobs in these sectors are more vulnerable than the same jobs in other countries.

It is believed that robots will take over because they are going to require less management than a human employee. However, on the same hand, while a robot is not getting paid salary or hourly, it still has to be maintained and upgraded whenever new programs come out. Therefore, is it really worth it?

Even if this were true, it is still a long way away because of the cost of robots, not to mention the moving of robots outside of a controlled environment is still a large step that has not been taken yet.

In the event of a robotic takeover, certain jobs are going to be safe. This does not mean that robots are not going to be used or help with these jobs, it just means that these jobs will not be fully taken over:

1. Athletes, sports instructors, sports officials
2. Firefighters, fire prevention, and fire inspection jobs
3. Yardmasters and railroad conductors
4. Fitness and recreation workers
5. Forest and conservation scientists
6. Public transportation attendants and inspectors (earlier in the book, there was mention of an automated bus. However, it is highly likely that these buses will have attendants on board in case the unexpected happens.)
7. Locomotive operators, engineers
8. Early school teachers, primary school teachers
9. Curators and archivists
10. Public servants, detectives, police
11. Airline pilots and navigators
12. Surveyors, cartographers, mapping scientists, and technicians
13. Actors, producers, directors
14. School bus drivers

Robotic Surgery

Robotic surgery is also known as robot-assisted surgery, and it allows surgeons to perform complicated procedures with more precision, control, and flexibility that they do not have when they are using conventional methods. Robotic surgery is going to be used mostly with minimally invasive surgeries that are going to be performed through a tiny incision. It is sometimes used with traditional open surgical procedures.

In 2000, robotic surgery first started with the FDA-approved da Vinci Surgery System. This technique was quickly adopted into medical centers over the United States and Europe to be used in treating a wide array of conditions.

This clinical robotic surgical system comes with a camera arm as well as a mechanical arm that has surgical instruments attached to it. The surgeon will control the arm while sitting at a computer console that is near the operating table. The console will provide the surgeon with a high definition, magnified, 3D view of what is going on in the surgical site.

Advantages

    1. fewer complications post-surgery

    2. smaller and less noticeable scars

    3. less pain and less blood loss during surgery

    4. Quicker recovery time.

Risks

    1. infections

    2. postoperative complications

Will robots take over the medical field?

Robots in the medical field are there to help enhance a doctor's skillset and make it safer for the patient when it comes to surgery. However, it is highly unlikely that systems such as the da Vinci are going to take the place of a human doctor.

Human doctors can provide a warm and caring nature that sets a patient's mind at ease, unlike a robot. Not to mention, in the event that there is a complication during surgery, a robot is not necessarily going to be trained to deal with it and that is when a surgeon is will step in and take care of what is going on without putting the patient in harm's way just to use an advanced piece of technology.

If anything, robotics is helping to advance medical technology by reducing the risks that patients are experiencing after they have gone through the surgery.

Also, humans enjoy talking to other humans, and that is not possible if there is not a human around to talk to. Robots do not have the bedside manner that human's do, which makes it to where they cannot provide the level of care that a patient wants from their surgeon.

This is why robotics will not take over surgery, but it will enhance a surgeon's skills so that they do not have to worry about losing a patient because they are not cutting open a patient and causing them to lose more blood than necessary.

Chapter 12: Robotics FAQ

There are many questions that people have about robotics, and in this chapter, we are going to answer some of the frequently asked questions that beginners have about robotics that were not answered earlier in this book.

1. What are some of the most commonly used sensor fusions algorithms seen in robotic multi-modeling sensing and how can they improve its position estimation by using a sensor fusion?

At this time, one of the best choices will be the Kalman filters as well as a particle filter. A Kalman filter will be useful whenever you are working with an initial position or linear measurements. The particle filter will be used even though the initial position is not known and there are no non-linear measurements. However, it will require a lot of computing that is not going to need to be done by the Kalman filters. No matter what sensor you are using, you will have to model the robot's states to estimate their propagation as well as update the estimations with any measurements that you have gotten.

2. Are robots going to be able to replace teachers?

No! Robots can do physical work and assist teachers in their lecture arrangements and management, which is why there are audio-video recording tools that teachers use. Nothing is going to be able to replace the relationship that a teacher builds with their students and their parents. It cannot display the same feelings of empathy that a teacher can show a student whenever that student is going through a rough time. In the end, a robot would be nothing more than a talking textbook.

3. What are some of the potential uses for artificial intelligence in the future?

Inside the scientific domains, there are more powerful computers that will be able to do what they are doing now except more faster thanks to an increase in processing power. These computers will help scientists discover significant patterns inside of large datasets. Computers are extremely useful tools not only for scientists but almost everyone in the world because of the access that they have to information that we otherwise would not have. When you look at the term artificial intelligence, computers are being used so that a better understanding of how the human brain is going to go through the process of making decisions is achieved. Knowing how a human brain makes decisions helps researchers and creators to make a robot that can follow the same process. When you look at how far AI has come already, it seems pretty believable that there are endless possibilities for AI in the future.

4. Is it possible that we are going to see a major role in the science of robotics come to teaching?

Yes. We have already seen how technology has helped teachers better teach their students, and robotics can come into play and help create a lesson plan that is going to target those students that are unable to learn in the ways that the teacher has been teaching his or her classes. Robotics can help teachers to personalize their classes and even better manage their time so that they can get to everything they want to when they are teaching for the year. Just like with the medical field, the possibilities of how robotics can help teachers is endless.

5. How are artificial intelligence and machine learning defined?

Artificial intelligence is the capabilities of a machine to imitate the intelligence that is seen in human behavior. AI technologies are nothing more than algorithms that will be trying to imitate what humans do. Machine learning, though, is the science and engineering that will provide computers with the ability to learn without having to be explicitly programmed.

6. Is intelligent assistance one of the only applications of artificial intelligence for customer care or are there other ways that artificial intelligence will impact customer service?

The front end use of AI technologies is going to make it to where intelligent assistants for customer care are the key, but there are multiple other applications at play as well. One thing will be the application for AI to directly support contact center agents rather than replacing them. Natural language and speech recognition will be used during live customer service interactions with a human agent to find relevant information and make suggestions for how the agent should respond.

7. Is there going to be a point in time where call centers are not necessary anymore?

As of right now? No. However, that can always change later on down the road depending on how technology can change thanks to robotics. The simpler tasks that can be handled through digital channels, thanks to various levels of automation, free up humans to deal with the more complex issues. Therefore, it is likely that robots and humans are going to work hand in hand in call centers.

8. What is the difference between Robotic process automation and artificial intelligence?

Before this question can be answered, you have to know the context. Should a company say, "We are planning on integrating artificial intelligence programs into our business processes," then they mean that they want to automate the process with a program's robot. In this case, RPA and AI will be the same thing.

In other situations, RPA solutions will automate processes with programs robots. These robots will be simple robots that do simple tasks, such as copying and pasting information into an Excel spreadsheet. Then, the more advanced RPA solutions will use machine learning to observe and learn how a human performs a task in order to automate it. Artificial intelligence describes a field of study that will try to automate human tasks like decision making. Therefore, RPA will use AI algorithms to perform complex tasks that have to have a degree of reasoning. There is an overlap in AI and RPA; however, not every RPA solution will be intelligent.

9. Why are experts looking into ethics when it comes to robotics?

Ever since the first factory robots were introduced into car manufacturing during the 1950s, they have become a part of modern life. Robots were popularized by science fiction films and books, and they are only now becoming more visible in modern societies.

Robots are now being used in factories all over the world. Drones are used in warfare while robots are being used to defuse bombs. Robots are beginning to replace workers in some service industries like shops and hotels. They can even be made to look like humans when caring for the elderly or being used in therapy for children with autism.

Robots (especially the humanoid ones) owe much of their popularity to literature and science fiction. The presence of robots in homes, the workplace and society are having an impact on human behavior. They also represent changes that have been made in society and cultures.

The report on methods will be aimed at trying to raise awareness about ethical issues that are tied to the use of autonomous robots in society.

10. How have robots been developed and how sophisticated could they be in the future?

When you look at the encyclopedia of Robotics, you will see that it distinguishes between five generations of robots. The first generation came about before 1980, and it was a mechanical, stationary piece of equipment that was precise, fast, and physically rugged. This robot did not have any external sensors or artificial intelligence.

The second generation was between 1980 and 1990, which had a microcomputer control and could be programmed. It also had vision systems, positions, and pressure sensors.

The third generation that came about in the mid-1990s and later was the autonomous and mobile robots, which could recognize and synthesize speech. These robots came with navigation systems or teleoperated artificial intelligence.

Finally, the fourth and fifth generations are the speculative roots that you will see in the future. These robots will acquire certain human characteristics, such as humor.

11. Why is the report looking at potential moral statuses of machines?

A robot's behavior – even if the robot is complex, autonomous, and intelligent – will be determined by a human.

However, if we assume that robots are most likely going to become more sophisticated in the future, then the nature of their algorithms will be an issue that is going to require attention from an ethics standpoint – concerning how robots should react and act in specific situations.

The problem with the development and utilization of robots is that other technological innovations cannot be planned or are not meant to happen, which can unintentionally harm humans.

It is likely that the malfunctioning of today's robots can cause much harm to many people.

In the end, the question becomes not only if robots have to be respected on certain ethical norms, but if certain norms have to be programmed into the actual robots. Such a need will be apparent should one focus on personal robots and the ways that they could cause harm to humans.

Robot autonomy is most likely going to grow to the point that their ethical regulation is going to be vital and they will need to be programmed with ethical codes that are invented specifically to prevent harmful behavior.

An intriguing question about robots that have enhanced autonomy and capacity for decision making brings up questions of their moral status.

Do robots deserve the same moral respect and immunity for the harm that is currently given to humans and animals?

Depending on the future advances in the research of robotics, you cannot exclude the possibility of a future robot's sentience, emotions, and even moral status. The rapid development of these highly intelligent autonomous robots will challenge the current classification of beings according to what their moral status is. Is it the same or is it going to be different in a profound way like what happened with the animal rights movement?

12. How is robotics going to be regulated?

Keep in mind that robots are complex beings, which raises the question as to who needs to be responsible for them both legally and ethically whenever the robots malfunction and hurt someone?

Robots, like other technologies, will be used for good and bad purposes. Robots continue to be under regulation both ethically and legally because they are still new and rapidly changing the field of research and the impact that they are going to have on the world cannot be anticipated.

There are not any specific guidelines on robotic research and projects, especially the ones that are having a direct impact on humans.

Also, there are no universally accepted codes of conduct for robotics. However, robots are treated the same way as other technological products when it comes to legal regulations.

13. It has been suggested that errors are going to happen because of humans and that it can confidently be said that there are not any quality issues with RPA whenever it is programmed by a human. Is this true?

The robotics programs work in a way that will follow the rules to the letter as told to it. It does not necessarily mean that there are not going to be any errors. During the early days of RPA, one of the first clients was involved with a telecommunications company that was able to program a robot that could send out iPhones to a customer that had ordered it. During the testing phase, there was a loop put in place to perform tests. When it finally went live they forgot to take out the loop; therefore, it sent everyone three to four phones. This is an example where issues can arise, and thus things fail on a large scale. That is why you have to be very careful when testing. No risk is going to forget a step at one stage.

14. What are some opportunity areas that clients may go after that are considered to be "low hanging fruit", and where do you see the next important ones?

RPA is not a process specific solution, and it is not the answer to everything. What it is, is the perfect tool for automating the gaps in the processes and systems being used. Whenever you are searching for opportunities that process, there is a good chance there will be a large number of people performing rule-based work and the data being inputted will have to be structured. Therefore, call centers are not suited for large-scale RPA and are better for the agent assisted solutions where the robots are on the agent's desk. In the event that you are looking to have more of an impact in automating a process, you should look to where people are handling data on a large scale – places like HR because they are vetting employees and doing payroll.

15. What is the cost to create and implement RPA solutions?

There is no price on the business case model; therefore, there is no overall practical price to be given. However, for more enterprises, there is a common range for single bot licenses which fall somewhere between $2,000 and $15,000 a year. But this is just for licenses which are only a small part of the overall cost of ownership. The robot can do the work of anything that you deploy. Should you be working normal business hours, then you are going to get a 1:1 ration in terms of one bot doing one FTE worth of work. However, if you are working 24/7, you can get 20 FTEs worth of that work. Whenever you look at the business cases for clients, it is common to see 500 to 800% ROIs over a period of three to five years.

Chapter 13: Machine Learning and Artificial Intelligence

Artificial intelligence is an up-and-coming field that is getting more and more popular as the days' pass. Artificial intelligence helps find solutions to things like where we want to eat, how to fix the global food shortage, and what the weather is going to be like tomorrow.

At first, artificial intelligence was just science fiction, and some people still think that it is nothing more than science fiction. However, there is going to be artificial intelligence around us every day, including that phone you use!

Take, for example, you are using an iPhone, and you hit the center button to ask Siri something. Well, guess what – Siri is artificial intelligence. So are the bank notifications that you get about possible fraudulent charges.

Intel's director of machine learning, Nidhi Chappell, has been reported saying, "Artificial intelligence is basically where machines make sense, learn, and interact with the external world without human beings having to specifically program it."

Artificial intelligence has not only made our lives easier, but it has improved it as well. Biometrics can measure how an athlete plays and how serious an injury is and how it will ultimately impact their playing time. On the other hand, farmers are using it so that they can know how much to water their crops so that they are getting the highest yield. Doctors are even using it so that they can detect diseases and track the treatment process of their patients.

You should think of the term artificial intelligence as an umbrella term that machine learning is going to fall under because of the various techniques and tools that will be used to allow a computer to think through mathematical algorithms that are based on the data that you have obtained. However, it is under this umbrella that you will also find machine learning's subset, which uses neural network models called deep learning that will use images so that they can be processed and recognized by the program that is being used.

"Think of a child growing up. That child observes the world, notes how people interact, learns society norms – without explicitly being told the rules," Chappell said. "That is the same as artificial intelligence. It is machines learning on their own without explicit programming."

It is also believed that artificial intelligence will be able to do at least three things:

1. Take action based on the recognition that it finds in the program.

2. Look at the world through any data patterns that can be detected.

3. Recognize patterns in the world around us.

Think of it like this. You are going to post a picture on Facebook. And because of facial recognition algorithms, Facebook is going to suggest that you tag friends in your photo so that they can see the photo as well. Not only that, but it is going to suggest pages and events based on the photo that you posted. So, if you post a picture of you and your best friend swimming at the lake, you are going to begin to see things that have to do with swimming because

Facebook's algorithm is going to assume that you like to swim based on the photo.

Machines are always going to try and get smarter, which is going to result in people making decisions faster and completing their research faster.

Assuaging Skeptics

People will always be skeptical of the things that they do not understand. This happens mainly because they are scared that machines are going to take over as depicted in the movie *Terminator*. However, Chappell has been reported saying that computers and the way that they learn is going to end up helping humanity in more ways than people are ever going to realize.

"Artificial intelligence actually augments what human beings are doing. We are not trying to replace humans. We are actually trying to augment them with more intelligence. This is making our lives easier."

Artificial intelligence makes it so that you no longer have to dig out a map to try and determine where you are and where you are going. All you have to do is put in the address, and a voice will tell you where you need to go. Not only that, but your phone will update each time the road changes so that you are not going somewhere that does not exist or using a road that is going to take longer for you to get down when there is a faster route.

Machine learning and artificial intelligence will be used in the fields of medicine, finance, and education. It will continue to keep society moving along without as much harassment that is found online. Another thing that artificial intelligence is going to help with is viruses such as Zika by looking at the mosquito population and determining which ones are most likely going to carry the disease.

Managing Data

Some of the most sophisticated learning will produce data which will require machines to learn. This means that the higher the computer is going to perform, the faster the computer will learn. "It is proven that the more data you give to a machine to learn, the more accurate the machine gets at predicting things," Chappell said about the complexity of how machines learn. The more complex the learning is, the more data requirements there are going to be.

Therefore, the more a computer learns, the more data requirements are going to be put into place.

When it all comes down to it, "artificial intelligence is around us everywhere," Ms. Diane Bryant, Intel Data Center Group's General Manager and Executive Vice President, said. "It is transforming the way that people engage with the world."

Conclusion

Thank you for making it through to the end of *Robotics*. It should have been informative and provided you with all of the tools needed to achieve your goals, whatever they may be.

The next step is to use the knowledge that you have gained here and either move on to learn more about robotics or to decide if you want robots in your life or not.

Not all robotics are evil, but it is up to you to do the research and figure out if it is something that you want to risk or not.

Robotics is in our lives everywhere, and as technology continues to develop, there is a chance that you will see robotics in your life even more. However, at the same time, with the advances that we have seen in technology, there is a chance that we will see the risks listed in this book not come to fruition.

No one knows what the future may hold, and you could be someone who helps to make robotics move forward and become even better than it already is!

Finally, if you found this book useful in any way, a review on Amazon is always appreciated!

Check out another book by Neil Wilkins

Printed in Great Britain
by Amazon